The Battle of Stalingrad

Books in the Battles Series:

The Attack on Pearl Harbor
The Battle of Antietam
The Battle of Belleau Wood
The Battle of Britain
The Battle of Gettysburg
The Battle of Hastings
The Battle of Marathon
The Battle of Midway

The Battle of Stalingrad
The Battle of Waterloo
The Battle of Zama
The Charge of the Light Brigade
Defeat of the Spanish Armada
The Inchon Invasion
The Invasion of Normandy
The Tet Offensive

★ ★ ★ **Battles of World War II** ★ ★ ★

The Battle
of Stalingrad

by Bob Carroll

Lucent Books, P.O. Box 289011, San Diego, CA 92198-9011

Library of Congress Cataloging-in-Publication Data

Carroll, Bob, 1936–
  The battle of Stalingrad / by Bob Carroll.
    p. cm. — (Battles of World War II)
  Includes bibliographical references and index.
  Summary: Describes the events surrounding the crucial World War II
battle in which Stalin's troops repulsed the Nazi invaders of the Soviet
Union.
  ISBN 1-56006-452-8 (alk. paper)
  1. Stalingrad, Battle of, 1942–1943—Juvenile literature.
[1. Stalingrad, Battle of, 1942–1943. 2. World War II, 1939–1945—
Campaigns—Soviet Union.] I. Title. II. Series.
D764.3.S7C38   1997
940.54'2147—dc20   96-30721
                                                             CIP
                                                             AC

Contents

Foreword 6

Chronology of Events 8

Introduction: The Significance of Stalingrad 9

Chapter 1: Two Roads to Tyranny 11

Chapter 2: Barbarossa 26

Chapter 3: Operation Blau 46

Chapter 4: Uranus 62

Chapter 5: On to Berlin 75

For Further Reading 89

Works Consulted 90

Index 91

Picture Credits 94

About the Author 95

Foreword

Almost everyone would agree with William Tecumseh Sherman that war "is all hell." Yet the history of war, and battles in particular, is so fraught with the full spectrum of human emotion and action that it becomes a microcosm of the human experience. Soldiers' lives are condensed and crystallized in a single battle. As Francis Miller explains in his *Photographic History of the Civil War* when describing the war wounded, "It is sudden, the transition from marching bravely at morning on two sound legs, grasping your rifle in two sturdy arms, to lying at nightfall under a tree with a member forever gone."

Decisions made on the battlefield can mean the lives of thousands. A general's pique or indigestion can result in the difference between life and death. Some historians speculate, for example, that Napoléon's fateful defeat at Waterloo was due to the beginnings of stomach cancer. His stomach pain may have been the reason that the normally decisive general was sluggish and reluctant to move his troops. And what kept George McClellan from winning battles during the Civil War? Some scholars and contemporaries believe that it was simple cowardice and fear. Others argue that he felt a gut-wrenching unwillingness to engage in the war of attrition that was characteristic of that particular conflict.

Battle decisions can be magnificently brilliant and horribly costly. At the Battle of Thaspus in 47 B.C., for example, Julius Caesar, facing a numerically superior army, shrewdly ordered his troops onto a narrow strip of land bordering the sea. Just as he expected, his enemy thought he had accidentally trapped himself and divided their forces to surround his troops. By dividing their army, his enemy had given Caesar the strategic edge he needed to defeat them. Other battle orders result in disaster, as in the case of the Battle of Balaclava during the Crimean War in 1854. A British general gave the order to attack a force of withdrawing enemy Russians. But confusion in relaying the order resulted in the 670 men of the Light Brigade's charging in the wrong direction into certain death by heavy enemy cannon fire. Battles are the stuff of history on the grandest scale—their outcomes often determine whether nations are enslaved or liberated.

Moments in battles illustrate the best and worst of human character. In the feeling of terror and the us-versus-them attitude that accompanies war, the enemy can be dehumanized and treated with a contempt that is considered repellent in times of peace. At Wounded Knee, the distrust and anticipation of violence that grew between the Native Americans and American soldiers led to the senseless killing of ninety men, women, and children. And who can forget My Lai, where the deaths of old men, women, and children at the hands of American soldiers shocked an America already disillusioned with the Vietnam War. The murder of six million Jews will remain burned into the human conscience forever as the measure of man's inhumanity to man. These horrors cannot be forgotten. And yet, under the terrible conditions of battle, one can find acts of bravery, kindness, and altruism. During the Battle of Midway, the members of Torpedo Squadron 8, flying in hopelessly antiquated planes and without the benefit of air protection from fighters, tried bravely to fulfill their mission—to destroy the *Kido Butai,* the Japanese Carrier Striking Force. Without air support, the squadron was immediately set upon by Japanese fighters. Nevertheless, each bomber tried valiantly to hit his target. Each failed. Every man but one died in the effort. But by keeping the Japanese fighters busy, the squadron bought time and delayed further Japanese fighter attacks. In the aftermath of the Battle of Isandhlwana in South Africa in 1879, a force of thousands of Zulu warriors trapped a contingent of British troops in a small trading post. After repeated bloody attacks in which many died on both sides, the Zulus, their final victory certain, granted the remaining British their lives as a gesture of respect for their bravery. During World War I, American troops were so touched by the fate of French war orphans that they took up a collection to help them. During the Civil War, soldiers of the North and South would briefly forget that they were enemies and share smokes and coffee across battle lines during the endless nights. These acts seem all the more dramatic, more uplifting, because they indicate that people can continue to behave with humanity when faced with inhumanity.

Lucent Books' Battles Series highlights the vast range of the human character revealed in the ordeal of war. Dramatic narrative describes in exciting and accurate detail the commanders, soldiers, weapons, strategies, and maneuvers involved in each battle. Each volume includes a comprehensive historical context, explaining what brought the parties to war, the events leading to the battle, what factors made the battle important, and the effects it had on the larger war and later events.

The Battles Series also includes a chronology of important dates that gives students an overview, at a glance, of each battle. Sidebars create a broader context by adding enlightening details on leaders, institutions, customs, warships, weapons, and armor mentioned in the narration. Every volume contains numerous maps that allow readers to better visualize troop movements and strategies. In addition, numerous primary and secondary source quotations drawn from both past historical witnesses and modern historians are included. These quotations demonstrate to readers how and where historians derive information about past events. Finally, the volumes in the Battles Series provide a launching point for further reading and research. Each book contains a bibliography designed for student research, as well as a second bibliography that includes the works the author consulted while compiling the book.

Above all, the Battles Series helps illustrate the words of Herodotus, the fifth-century B.C. Greek historian now known as the "father of history." In the opening lines of his great chronicle of the Greek and Persian Wars, the world's first battle book, he set for himself this goal: "To preserve the memory of the past by putting on record the astonishing achievements both of our own and of other peoples; and more particularly, to show how they came into conflict."

Chronology of Events

1939

August 23 USSR and Germany sign nonaggression pact.

1941

June 22 Germany invades USSR in Operation Barbarossa.

1942

August 23 German army units enter northern suburbs of Stalingrad.

Russian troops stand amidst bombed-out buildings in Stalingrad.

Early September German advances gradually grind to a halt.

September 9 Hitler fires General Wilhelm List, personally takes command of the army.

September 12 Vasily Chuikov named commander of forces inside Stalingrad.

September 17–20 Fierce struggle for grain elevator on southern outskirts of city.

September 24 Colonel-General Franz Halder relieved of command.

October Intense street fighting; neither side can gain victory but Russians continue to hang on.

October 31 Russians launch partially successful counterattack and retake part of tractor factory.

Early November Volga River begins to freeze over.

November 11 Germans launch yet another unsuccessful major attack.

November 19 Russian counterattack, code-named Uranus, begins.

November 22 Russians encircle German Sixth Army.

December 9 German Fourth Panzer Army ordered to relieve the Sixth Army; the first two German soldiers starve to death in Stalingrad.

December 25 German Sixth Army celebrates a bleak Christmas.

1943

January 1 Widespread starvation and illness among German troops.

January 30 Friedrich Paulus promoted to field marshal.

January 31 German Sixth Army surrenders at Stalingrad.

Ignoring the body of a dead German, a Nazi general leads his defeated division out of Stalingrad after the surrender of the Sixth Army.

July 4 Germans open disastrous assault on Kursk.

INTRODUCTION

The Significance of Stalingrad

Clutching their only belongings, Russian women walk through the ruins of Stalingrad, razed by German attacks.

There is no Stalingrad today. What Adolf Hitler could not do in 1942, Russian anti-Stalinism accomplished in 1961. When at last the great mass of Russian people learned of the brutalities and butcheries committed by their former dictator, the city that bore his name was officially renamed Volgograd. By then, of course, nearly twenty years had elapsed since the cataclysmic battle that put the name of the city in headlines worldwide. Stalin himself had been dead for almost a decade.

For seven hundred years, from the time it was founded in the 1200s, the city was called Tsaritsyn, but the tsar—the Russian ruler—and his family were unseated and eventually murdered during the Russian Revolution of 1917. The new communist Union of Soviet Socialist Republics (USSR) tolerated no place-names honoring former royalty. Petrograd, the capital city under the tsars, became Leningrad for Vladimir Ilich Lenin, the chief leader of the revolution and head of the communist government until 1924. In 1925, when Joseph Stalin succeeded Lenin to power, he renamed Tsaritsyn Stalingrad after himself.

In the fall and winter of 1942, Stalingrad became the site of a tremendous, last-ditch battle that was the single greatest turning point of World War II. One bloodstained dictator, Stalin, turned back the aggression of another, Adolf Hitler. The Battle of Stalingrad marked the beginning of the USSR's and the other

Allies' path to victory in World War II. Taking place over several months and involving millions of people, the battle was extremely complex, but its significance is simplicity itself: until Stalingrad, Hitler and Nazi Germany were winning the war; after Stalingrad, they were losing.

How the battle was fought can be understood only by studying the personalities of Stalin and Hitler, because the fight for the city was more important to each of them than any strategic advantage could warrant. Stalingrad became a test of wills between the two dictators.

The city's name, however ill deserved, was part of the story of the battle. To Hitler, the German führer, it came to symbolize his greatest enemy, Stalin himself. And, mesmerized by the symbolic importance of Stalingrad more than by the strategic importance of the city, Hitler made emotional decisions that were militarily irrational. As a result, he sealed his own destruction.

For the USSR, Stalingrad marked the beginning of the Soviet Union's rise from an overgrown and meddlesome gadfly on the world scene to its position as one of the two superpowers that shaped the world in the second half of the twentieth century.

CHAPTER ONE

Two Roads to Tyranny

Hitler's and Stalin's personal quirks heavily influenced World War II, and especially the Battle of Stalingrad. Historians argue over which of the two dictators was the supreme mass murderer of the twentieth century. Each bears direct responsibility for the deaths of millions of innocent people and, indirectly, for those of millions more who died on the battlefields of World War II. And, though Adolf Hitler deserves most of the blame for launching that war, he was able to do so only with the connivance of Joseph Stalin. Of all history's tyrants, these two rank among the most detestable ever unleashed on the world.

Yet they were very different in many of their character traits. Hitler built his career on anticommunism, racial hatred, and German greed. Mercurial and charismatic, his political and military decisions were as often as not based on hunches, guesses, or wishful thinking rather than sound strategy. Nevertheless, by his very audaciousness, he was at first successful. His string of early successes created a belief in his infallibility among the German people as well as in his own mind. When things did not go his way, usually because reality conflicted with his desires, he could fly into towering rages, accusing even his most ardent supporters of treason. His bombastic speeches, filled with theatrical gestures and dramatic pronouncements, may appear staged and even funny to modern audiences who see them on film, but they inspired the German citizens of his time as no oratory had done before. In the words of Colonel Red Reeder in his book *The Story of the Second World War*, Hitler "sowed hatred to bind his people together, and made most of his countrymen believe he

In his blind determination to crush Stalingrad, Adolf Hitler often made his military decisions based on emotion rather than sound strategy.

could build a new order that would last a thousand years."

Hitler played on his followers' emotions and was emotion-led himself. Stalin, on the other hand, never let his emotions govern him. He distrusted everyone. Although his decisions were sometimes based on his almost paranoid distrust, they were never swayed by compassion. He seemed incapable of pity. Unlike Hitler, his personality could never inspire loyalty, much less adulation; rather, he came to absolute power through an unholy combination of deceit, cruelty, and clear-eyed pragmatism. Hitler called him "an ice-cold blackmailer." The Russian despot was plodding, icy, and crude, with no personal charm at all, but those cold-blooded qualities were his strength. He let nothing stand in the way of his bloody path to dictatorship.

Stalin Comes to Power

In Russia the horrible suffering caused by World War I brought on a revolution and the beginning of Stalin's rise. In Germany, anger over the war's outcome and resentment of the peace terms created a climate in which Hitler could thrive. The so-called war to end all wars set both Russia and Germany on the road to an even more deadly conflict.

In 1914 Russia entered World War I on the side of Britain and France against the Central Powers led by Germany. The ordinary Russian soldier was poorly trained, badly equipped, and poorly led by officers who owed their rank to noble birth rather than skill. Battle after battle was lost with staggering casualties. Wave after wave of troops marched into battle, many without ammunition, some without even rifles. They were cut down mercilessly, yet their unskilled officers knew no other strategy but to order another attack. Meanwhile, on the home front, the lack of manpower and raw materials produced ever greater deprivation and suffering. Necessities were in short supply and prices soared while wages stayed low. Paper money became almost worthless. Soon farmers, unwilling to accept payment in paper, refused to send food into the cities. The people blamed the tsar, Nicholas II, for the war and all its hardships.

Early in 1917 a series of riots over food shortages and strikes over working conditions convinced Nicholas that he could no longer govern, and he abdicated. The Bolsheviks, political extremists comprising only a tiny fragment of the population, were

Communists and Nazis

The doctrines of communism and Nazism were in direct opposition to each other, but they had much in common. Both were political-economic systems that claimed to have the interests of ordinary people at heart. Both were totalitarian—they controlled all facets of society. And both communists and Nazis maintained their power by their ability to terrorize and destroy their opponents.

The origins of communism are to be found in the writings of Karl Marx, a nineteenth-century German who believed that all of human history was dictated by economics. He said that capitalism, the prevailing economic system in which the means of production such as factories and mines were privately owned, must be abolished. Ownership of the means of production must be placed in the hands of the workers. He differed from socialists, who also called for an end to private ownership, in that he insisted capitalists would never willingly give up control. The workers could only triumph, according to Marx, by way of revolution.

Vladimir Ilich Lenin, who established the world's first communist government in Russia, set about putting the means of production under state ownership, but he changed Marx's theories in one crucial way. Instead of political and economic control by the workers, he vested all power in the Communist Party, which claimed to represent the workers. The communists allowed no opposition. The only legal political party was the Communist Party and its power was enforced by the secret police. The Communist Party also controlled the media and the arts. Under Stalin, the control of the state was drawn even more tightly into the hands of a single dictator.

Unlike communism, Nazism encouraged private ownership but that ownership was held under strict control and followed the desires of the state, which was led by an all-powerful dictator. As Nazism grew in Germany, many industrialists backed Hitler, and grew rich in the process. They mistakenly believed at first that they controlled Hitler. Only later did they realize that they were completely under his thumb.

The Fascists, led by Benito Mussolini, achieved power in Italy before the Nazis did in Germany, and therefore Nazism is sometimes said to be a fascist form of government, but they are simply two sides to the same coin. Both systems persecute minorities, are extremely nationalistic, and advocate war to achieve national aims.

Rows of German soldiers march holding banners emblazoned with swastikas, the Nazi Party symbol.

given no part in the democratic government that replaced him. Under Lenin's direction, they refused to cooperate with the new government and retaliated with more strikes and riots. The government played into the Bolsheviks' hands by stubbornly continuing the war and insisting that badly needed reforms on the home front be put off until the conflict ended. The Bolsheviks, by contrast, promised immediate peace and instant reform.

By the fall, conditions had worsened, in part as a result of the Bolsheviks' continued insurrections. On November 7, Lenin and the Bolsheviks accomplished a coup and took control of the government.

As soon as they were in office, the Bolsheviks sued for peace with Germany, as they had promised. The Germans, knowing that the Bolshevik position was precarious, imposed harsh terms, and the actual peace agreement was not signed until the following spring. Britain, France, and the United States strongly opposed the new Russian government and attempted whenever possible to undermine it. They knew that peace on the Russian front meant the Germans could redirect thousands of soldiers who had been facing Russia to fight the Allies in France. Furthermore, the avowed aim of Marxism was to spread communist revolution throughout the world, including the Western democracies.

Frustrated by the state of their country, revolutionaries organize to take over the government. After the Russian Revolution, the new government agreed to the harsh terms set forth by Germany in order to reach a peace settlement.

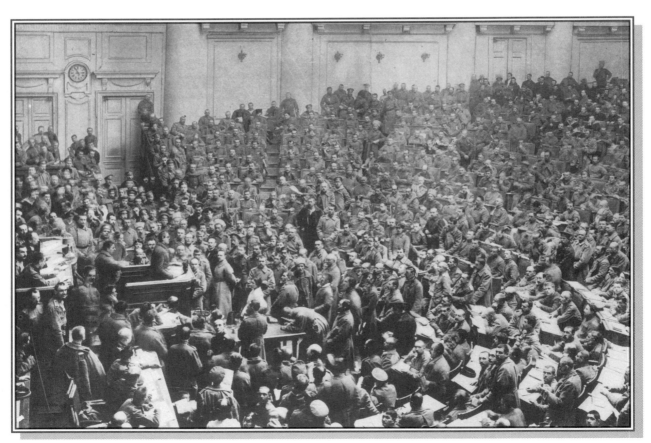

In addition to signing a separate peace with Germany, the Bolsheviks began the process of nationalizing the country by turning over many large estates held by the wealthy and by the church to collectives of the peasants who worked on them. Workers in some industries were allowed to manage their factories and shops, although ultimate ownership and control of industry and land rested with the state.

Lenin ran the country as chairman of a fifteen-man committee called the Soviet of the People's Commissars. *Soviet* is a Russian word meaning "council." In 1922 Russia and a number of small countries under its control officially became the Union of Soviet Socialist Republics, or USSR. The commissar for nationalities on the Soviet of People's Commissars was Joseph Stalin.

Stalin, originally Iosif Vissarionovich Dzhugashvili, was born in 1879 in the small town of Gori in Georgia, the southernmost province of what then was the Russian empire. His father was a poor shoemaker and a drunkard who treated his son cruelly. His mother worked as a washerwoman to earn money for Iosif's education. He was a bright student and earned a scholarship to a religious seminary, where he studied for the priesthood. But he was attracted to Marxist theories. In 1898 he joined a secret Marxist group. Within a year, he was expelled from the seminary.

Iosif began organizing antitsarist strikes and protests in southern Russia and writing rebellious articles for underground newspapers. In 1902 he was arrested by the tsar's secret police and eventually exiled to Siberia. He was still there the following year when the Bolsheviks under Lenin split from other communist organizations. In 1904 he escaped from Siberia and returned to his underground activities. He was recaptured and spent seven of the next ten years either in jail or in exile. In 1913, in part to avoid the secret police, he took the name of Stalin from a Russian word meaning "man of steel."

He had met Lenin in 1905 and apparently impressed the Bolshevik leader. Seven years later, Lenin named him to the party's Central Committee over better-known candidates. Lenin also helped him write a long article called "The National Question and Social Democracy" and made him one of the editors of *Pravda* (*Truth*), the Bolshevik newspaper.

Stalin was again in exile in Siberia when the tsar abdicated in 1917, but the new government freed most political prisoners. He hurried west to play a part in November's Bolshevik coup, though he was by no means as important to the outcome as Lenin or the brilliant Leon Trotsky, then considered second only to Lenin in the Bolshevik ranks.

Vladimir Ilich Lenin, who took control of the Russian government after the Bolshevik coup, stands to the left of revolutionary leader Leon Trotsky (saluting) at a 1919 parade in Moscow's Red Square.

During their first years in power, the Bolsheviks faced several armed uprisings by dissidents calling for a less radical government, some of whom even advocated the return of a tsar. Trotsky distinguished himself in leading the Bolsheviks to eventual victory. Stalin was active militarily in southern Russia, though in no sense was he as important as revisionist history books later claimed.

During the civil wars, the Bolsheviks established the five-member Politburo as the policy-making body of the government. Lenin had Stalin elected as one of the five. In 1922, again under Lenin's directive, he was named general secretary of the party.

But Lenin began to have misgivings about Stalin. He was repelled by Stalin's rude ways and he suspected that the general secretary was abusing his office by placing his supporters in key positions and limiting opportunities for those who opposed him. Lenin wrote a secret note that Stalin must be removed from office, but before he could take action, his health failed. The note was not revealed to other Bolshevik leaders until after Lenin's death in 1924.

The logical successor to Lenin was Trotsky, his charismatic second-in-command. Trotsky was a man of ideas who had shown himself to be an excellent military leader as well during the civil wars. But Stalin, from his position as general secretary, was able to block Trotsky by systematically removing his supporters from positions of power and replacing them with men loyal to himself. In fear for his life, Trotsky fled the country in 1929. Eleven years later he was murdered in Mexico City under Stalin's order.

A Reign of Terror

Karl Marx had advocated a dictatorship of the workers; Lenin changed that to a dictatorship of a few party leaders. Stalin reduced the dictatorship to one man—himself.

At the age of fifty, Stalin had become absolute dictator of the USSR, the largest nation on earth. No one in the Soviet Union dared criticize him. Under the tsars, the secret police had often arrested and exiled revolutionaries. They were feared, but not nearly so much as were Stalin's secret police. Anyone suspected of opposing Stalin, of helping those who opposed him, or even of criticizing him was likely to be arrested. Many were jailed without trial, many more were exiled to Siberia, and untold thousands simply disappeared, never to be seen again. When trials were held, the accused always confessed to plotting against the state. Those who informed on others' acts of "treason" were considered heroes and given favorable treatment—at least until someone else informed on them. Friends of many years found they could no longer trust one another. Even children were encouraged to inform on their parents.

At the top of Stalin's hate list were the old Bolsheviks who had been close to Lenin. They had been comrades of Stalin, too, of course, and many of them had helped him gain power. But Stalin's only loyalty was to himself. He feared not only that the old heroes of the revolution might somehow instigate another revolution but also that one or more of them might reveal his secrets. They were arrested and, in a series of trials staged and scripted for propaganda purposes, confessed to all manner of subversive acts. By 1935, in systematic purges, most of them had been eliminated. Next, because Stalin feared the military might try to remove him, the Soviet army was purged of most of its senior officers. This move would backfire, however, when war broke out and Stalin found his army with virtually no veteran leaders.

As horrible as was Stalin's use of the secret police, it paled beside the misery and deaths caused by his economic policies. Starting in 1928, he instituted a series of five-year plans designed to bring the country economically into the twentieth century. Private ownership of business and industry was eliminated. The government dictated what and how much would be manufactured. Production of industrial machinery and heavy farm equipment grew but ordinary items such as clothing and household goods suffered. While tractors poured off the assembly line, the worker who built them stood in line for hours to buy an overpriced pair of shoes. A toaster could cost several weeks' wages.

The lot of peasants was worse. Stalin ordered the collectivization of Soviet agriculture. All private farms, along with their equipment and livestock, were to be combined into giant state-run farms. A peasant could no longer own a small plot of land, a tractor, or even a cow. Everything belonged to the state. The peasants resisted, withholding their produce and even slaughtering their own animals. This caused widespread starvation in the cities. Stalin had about a million peasants exiled to Siberia; many were simply murdered. The peasants who remained were completely cowed. Although farm production eventually surpassed pre–World War I levels, the cost in individual lives was staggering.

Stalin also adopted the policy of Russification, first begun by the tsars. Under this policy, minority nationalities within the Soviet Union were subjected to strict controls, deprived of property, excluded from certain vocations, and generally treated as second-class citizens.

Stalin saw the industrialized countries of the West as his greatest enemies and as the greatest threat to his dictatorship. He was convinced that leaders in Paris, London, and Washington were plotting his overthrow. To some extent he was right.

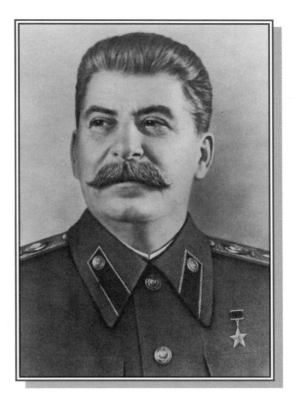

Dictatorial leader Joseph Stalin drove Russia into misery with his failed economic policies and his use of the brutal secret police.

The Western democracies had not forgiven the Bolsheviks for taking Russia out of World War I. They believed that their road to victory had been made much more difficult once Germany could concentrate its armies against the West. But more importantly, they feared communism as the avowed enemy of both democracy and capitalism. When the Bolsheviks first gained control in Russia, they fully expected their revolution to spread quickly to the Western industrialized nations. They were wrong. Conditions for workers or poor farmers in Great Britain or the United States, for example, were never quite as bad as those in Russia. Moreover, the industrialized nations had traditions of democracy; most of their people considered the USSR's lack of individual freedom intolerable. Nevertheless, in each industrialized nation there were always a few who believed in the communist ideal and hoped to establish a so-called workers' paradise in their own country. The USSR encouraged such homegrown communists, and, to a large extent, communists around the world followed the dictates of Moscow. Small wonder then that the Western democracies at first treated the USSR as an outlaw. Even after more normal relations between the Soviet Union and the West were established, neither side believed the other could be trusted.

Although the USSR's relations with Britain, France, and the United States were strained, Stalin found a more ruthless enemy much closer to his doorstep in the 1930s, when Germany began to grow in power. He knew that Hitler was far more likely to attack than any of the democracies and set out unsuccessfully to arrange mutual assistance pacts with the British and French. When the Spanish army under General Francisco Franco rebelled against the king and sought to set up a military dictatorship in 1936, the USSR sent advisers and equipment to the Loyalists. The world was treated to the inconceivable: communists defending royalty! Meanwhile, Hitler and Italian dictator Benito Mussolini aided Franco and helped him to victory. If nothing else, the Spanish civil war showed that German equipment and leadership was superior to that of the Soviets. Anti-Hitler propaganda as delivered by *Pravda* and other communist-controlled organs became ever more virulent.

Then suddenly, without warning, on August 23, 1939, the USSR and Germany signed a mutual nonaggression pact. The world gaped in disbelief—the communist dictator and the führer were allied! *Pravda* made a U-turn and began to praise Hitler as a statesman. There was precious little time to reflect on what it meant. That became clear a week later when Germany began World War II.

Hitler's Rise

Stalin became dictator of the USSR by working secretly behind the scenes; Adolf Hitler's rise to German leadership was played out more publicly. Whereas Stalin was virtually unknown to most

Russians until he gained power and certainly owed no part of his position to "the will of the people," Hitler was a familiar public figure in Germany for years before he became "der Führer." Indeed, without the support of at least a portion of the German voters, he could never have come to power at all.

He was born in 1889 not in Germany but just across the Austrian border in the town of Braumau. His father, a customs official, was harsh and ill tempered, demanding the boy give up his constant daydreaming and drawing and work harder in school. His mother spoiled him. Soon after his father died in 1903, Adolf left school. His mother's pension enabled him to spend his time making pictures instead of finding a job. In 1907 he went to Vienna, the artistic center of Austria, determined to become an artist. He was able to live comfortably and occasionally sell a painting, but his dreams of success were set back when he twice failed the entrance exam to the Academy of Fine Arts. His artwork was competent but lacked originality or flair. Hitler, however, blamed others for his failures, particularly Jews.

With the outbreak of World War I, Hitler enlisted in the German army. Though Austrian by birth, he had become a fierce German nationalist. He served most of the war on the western front, fought in several of the deadliest battles, and was twice wounded. Though decorated for bravery, he never rose above the rank of corporal.

The armistice in 1918 shocked Hitler as it did many Germans. At the time, they believed the German army was winning. The German leaders, however, knew the truth: The army was about to collapse from exhaustion, lack of replacements in men and weapons, and the Allies' superior manpower and manufacturing capabilities once the United States entered the war on the Allies' side. Germany accepted peace to avoid invasion.

A 1918 armistice among nations ended Germany's involvement in World War I. The agreement shocked many German citizens, who wrongly believed their country had been winning the war.

After the war, many Germans blamed betrayal on the home front for the loss. The German army had never before been defeated. At the root of the treason were Jews and communists, they insisted. The Treaty of Versailles, the peace agreement, also rankled. It blamed Germany for the war and exacted huge reparations (payments) for war damages. Another betrayal, screamed the nationalists, calling for prosecution of the "criminals" who signed it.

In 1919 in the city of Munich, Hitler joined a small group of extreme nationalists who called themselves the National Socialist German Workers Party. They would soon become better known as Nazis. The Nazis called for the union of all Germanic nations into one greater Germany. Only pure-blooded Germans were entitled to citizenship. All other races, particularly Jews and Slavs, were inferior and useful only as servants of the so-called master race. In their warped philosophy, communists, Jews, and other inferiors were at the root of all Germany's ills.

The Nazis' hate-filled message came at the right time for Germans looking for scapegoats. The terms of the peace treaty were universally resented. The economy was in a shambles and inflation was rising. People had little faith that the newly seated democratic government could solve their problems. As desperation increased, even otherwise rational Germans were willing to listen to Nazi promises to restore their country to world power. In Italy, which faced many of the same problems, dictator Benito Mussolini was able to capture the government. Might not Germany be ready for a similar solution?

Hitler soon rose to the leadership of the Nazi Party. He was an able politician and a good organizer. Moreover, his angry speeches were effectively rallying many of his frustrated countrymen to the Nazi banner. In 1923 he led an attempted overthrow of the local Bavarian government. The plot failed and he was sentenced to prison.

Hitler sits among a group of loyal followers. Germans, desperate for a better life after the devastating effects of World War I, accepted Hitler's hate-filled ideals, and the ambitious leader quickly rose within the leadership of the Nazi Party.

The Beer Hall Putsch

In 1923 Adolf Hitler made an unsuccessful grab for power in the city of Munich. A series of strikes protesting rocketing inflation caused the government in Berlin to place the country in a state of emergency. In Bavaria, the local government came under the control of three men: the state commissioner and the heads of the local army and police. Upon learning that all three planned to speak at a meeting of civil servants to be held at the Burgerbraukeller, a Munich beer hall, Hitler decided to make his move.

In the midst of the meeting, he strode into the hall accompanied by Göring and several bodyguards, leaped on a table, and fired a pistol into the ceiling. Then, while his men set up a machine gun, he announced to the startled assembly that the revolution had begun, the building was surrounded by six hundred heavily armed men, and police and soldiers were marching into the city under the Nazi banner. It was pure bluff, but those in the room had no way of knowing that. Göring told them not to worry and to keep drinking their beer. Meanwhile, Hitler took the three leaders of the government into an adjoining room and tried to bully and threaten them into handing him control of Bavaria.

Eventually, the three leaders were able to slip away after Hitler left to speak to General Erich Ludendorff, a hero of World War I. Hitler planned to use him as a figurehead in his revolutionary government. Although Ludendorff was not a Nazi, he was sympathetic to their racist and nationalistic cause.

The next morning, Hitler and Ludendorff led about two thousand storm troopers and hangers-on in a march into Munich. Along the way they sang and chanted slogans. The first time they were stopped by the police, Göring threatened to shoot some supposed hostages held in the rear of the parade, and they were allowed to pass. But as they approached a second police roadblock in the heart of the city, shots rang out. Sixteen marchers and three policemen were killed. Hitler came away without a wound, although his shoulder was slightly injured when the man next to him and with whom he had linked arms fell with a bullet in his head. According to many accounts, the future führer was among the first to run for his life. Ludendorff stood straight and waited to be arrested.

The treason trial was a farce. The court sided with the accused. Ludendorff was acquitted outright. Hitler used the trial to make bombastic speeches that helped make him a national figure. He was convicted but only with the assurance that he would not serve the full five years his offense required. He spent nine months in prison.

While in prison, Hitler wrote *Mein Kampf* (*My Struggle*), in which he laid out his plans for Germany's future. In what might be seen as a warning to the world, Hitler wrote that all the lands Germany had controlled before World War I must be returned and that Austria and those parts of Czechoslovakia where Germans lived must become part of Germany. Moreover, this greater Germany must have lebensraum, or living space, accomplished by taking land from Poland and the Soviet Union. According to Hitler, a democratic government must inevitably fall to communism, so the current government must be superseded by a Nazi dictatorship that could deal ruthlessly with the communists. Much of the book was given over to the Nazi doctrine of the master race and to blaming the Jews for every wrong found anywhere in the world.

When Hitler was released from prison in 1924, he returned to his political agenda, but this time more carefully. Over the next several years, he slowly rebuilt his party and convinced the government, which had outlawed the Nazis, that its members would act responsibly and legally. He toned down some of his more inflammatory oratory to appeal to a wider base of voters.

To Hitler's advantage, democracy in Germany was threatened by the economic depression that struck worldwide at the beginning of the 1930s. Unemployment soared while inflation rose to new heights. Hunger was rampant. Many people were willing to accept desperate remedies.

In the elections of 1932 the Nazis received more than a third of the votes, making them the largest party in Germany though far from a majority. Hitler was offered several cabinet posts, but he would accept only the position of chancellor, or prime minister. Certainly the majority of Germans did not want that, not with Hitler's record of advocating a dictatorship. On the other hand, a stable government could not be formed without the participation of Germany's largest party. Unfortunately, the German president, Paul von Hindenburg, was eighty-five years old and in failing health. Tired and sick, he was willing to accept Hitler's promises that he would rule lawfully. On January 30, 1933, he named Hitler chancellor. The key to the chicken coop had been handed to the fox.

After accepting the office of chancellor of Germany in 1933 (pictured), Hitler set his sights on gaining absolute power.

The Nazis still lacked a majority of cabinet positions or representatives in the Reichstag, the German legislature. Then, on February 27, the Reichstag building burned. Most historians believe the Nazis started the fire, but the Nazis blamed the communists and used that accusation as a pretext to refuse the communist delegates the seats in the legislature they had won in the election. That gave the Nazis the majority they needed to push through sweeping laws that suspended civil rights and made Hitler dictator—the führer—of Germany.

The Road to War

As soon as he gained control, Hitler secretly began to rearm Germany for the war he planned. By 1936 he felt Germany was strong enough that he could openly build his army in violation of the Treaty of Versailles. As he expected, to avoid war, the other nations of Europe did nothing to stop him. In further violation of the treaty, he moved troops into the Rhineland, that part of Germany west of the Rhine River. Again, the nations of Europe sat back and allowed him a free hand. Nor was anything done when he sent troops and equipment to Spain to support General Franco in that country's civil war. In March 1938 Germany annexed Austria; Austrian leaders who admired Hitler paved the way so that German troops were allowed to invade the country with little opposition.

With each step, the German generals expected war to begin, but Hitler knew that England and France, the only nations likely to oppose him militarily, were not ready to fight. They had disarmed after World War I and by the mid-1930s lagged far behind Germany militarily. Europe followed a policy of appeasement, making concessions in hope that Hitler would be satisfied. Hitler, for his part, preceded each new demand with promises—lies—that this was the last demand he would make.

In September 1938, tensions came to a head over the Sudetenland, that part of Czechoslovakia in which German was spoken. Hitler alleged that Germans were being mistreated there and insisted that those areas be turned over to Germany. This, he swore, would be his final demand. Although France and England had pledged to protect Czechoslovakia's territorial integrity, they backed down once more at a meeting in Munich and handed the Sudetenland to Hitler. Neville Chamberlain, the British prime minister, told his countrymen that the Munich agreement had achieved "peace in our time." A few months later, Germany gobbled up the rest of Czechoslovakia.

Hitler had thus already greatly expanded Germany without going to war, but his next step was certain to force England and France to take up arms. He was ready to begin acquiring the lebensraum he had long coveted by invading Poland. But England

Hermann Göring

The roll call of villains in the Nazi hierarchy could fill a book. One man was most closely associated with Hitler in the public's mind: Hermann Göring.

Before the war, much of the world thought of stout Hermann Göring (1893–1946) as the Nazis' comic relief. Indeed, photos and newsreels showing his round build and apparent joviality, along with his love of extravagant entertainments, elegant debaucheries, and elaborate uniforms festooned with medals and colorful decorations, made him seem more clown than villain to many. But Göring had a darker, less public side. Ruthless and brutal with any who opposed him, he was a key figure in Hitler's rise, and as the number-two Nazi had his hand in all of the decisions that led to millions of deaths.

In the early days of National Socialism, Göring was far more famous than Hitler. During World War I, he had been a flying ace and served as the last commander of the squadron once led by the "Red Baron," Manfred von Richthofen. Coming from a wealthy family, he helped the early Nazi movement with personal loans and his prestige as a war hero. He became one of Hitler's earliest confidants. In 1928 he was one of the first Nazis elected to the Reichstag, the German legislature. Eventually, he became its president and used his position to pave the way for Hitler to come to power.

During the 1930s he oversaw the buildup of Germany's armament industry as the Nazis prepared for war. Hitler made him commander of the Luftwaffe, the German air force, and, as Reichsmarschall, he was second in power only to the führer himself.

But Göring was a braggart. He promised his Luftwaffe would bring England to its knees, and he announced that Allied airplanes would never bomb Berlin. His vain boast that he could supply the German army at Stalingrad by air contributed to the defeat. When he was proved wrong on all counts, his power began to wane.

Hermann Göring's barbarous tactics and fierce loyalty to the führer landed him the second most powerful position in the Nazi Party.

and France had signed a mutual defense pact with the Poles. After so many lies by Hitler, they realized that their appeasement policy had failed. If Hitler moved against Poland, war was inevitable.

Hitler hesitated. He believed he could conquer Poland easily and then turn all his force on England and France. However, there was one large problem—the Soviet Union. An invasion of Poland was certain to cause the USSR to oppose him. Though the Russian colossus was on his timetable of conquest, Hitler did not want to fight a two-front war—England and France to the west, the USSR to the east.

Stalin had no doubt that the Soviet Union was on Hitler's menu, but his attempts to forge a defense pact with the western Allies had failed. Now he turned to Germany, his avowed enemy. He reasoned that by becoming Hitler's ally, he could put off a German invasion for years, at least until Russia had built up its army and armaments. When Hitler threw in a bonus—Germany secretly agreed to share conquered Poland with the Soviet Union—the deal was struck.

Germany and the USSR signed a pact that pledged mutual cooperation and neutrality in case either went to war against another country. That left Hitler free to start his war, certain in the knowledge that he could deal with the western Allies without fearing Russia at his back. It was an agreement made in hell, for it made World War II possible. Within a week of its signing, German troops poured across the border into Poland.

Carrying out Hitler's plan to expand German territory, Nazi troops roll through the easily acquired Sudetenland in 1938.

CHAPTER TWO

Barbarossa

When Germany invaded Poland in 1939, the Nazi propaganda machine explained Hitler's act by arguing that on August 31, 1939, an aggressive Poland viciously invaded a peaceful and unsuspecting Germany. An armed Polish army unit crossed the border and was only kept from marching all the way to Berlin by the prompt and courageous actions of German defenders.

As proof of Polish aggression, foreign journalists were taken to a small forest near Hochlinde, about ten miles from the border, and shown a dozen dead bodies dressed in Polish military uniforms. These men, they were told, had been killed when German border guards staunchly repelled the attack.

Masses of German panzers launch a blitzkrieg attack on Poland in 1939, setting World War II in motion.

To shore up their absurd scenario, the Nazis staged an elaborate charade. On the same day the Nazis said Poland invaded Germany, August 31, a half dozen men wearing civilian clothes commandeered a small German radio station near the German-Polish border at Gleiwitz. Speaking Polish, the supposed leader of the force broadcast the news of the invasion of Germany and called upon all Poles to join in the attack. Listeners then heard a fusillade of shots as, apparently, German security troops arrived.

Citing these two acts of aggression by Poland, Nazi propagandists explained that peace-loving Germans led by brave Adolf Hitler had no option but to launch a defensive action against the treacherous Poles.

Of course, it was all a sham. After all, it was Hitler who advised never tell a little lie when a big one will do.

The dozen "Polish invaders" were in fact condemned German prisoners who had been forced into Polish uniforms and herded to that spot in the woods, where they were shot. Their bodies were then arranged so as to make it appear they had been advancing into Germany. A dead man at the radio station was another prisoner, but he was not the one who had broadcast the call to arms. That voice had belonged to one of six Hitler henchmen who had taken over the station and staged the mock on-air gun battle. The prisoner's only part in the activity was to provide his dead body as "evidence." The whole plan—the bodies in the forest and the false radio broadcast—had been code-named Operation Canned Goods.

The actual details of this preposterous invasion story were not known until after the war, but even at the time only the most credulous believed such poppycock. The whole charade was nothing more than Hitler's pretext for invading a peaceful neighbor. In the hours before dawn on September 1, less than a day after the sham Polish attack, Hitler unleashed his military might on Poland, and began World War II.

Poland Is Overrun

It was a mismatch from the start. Hitler sent 1.5 million troops into Poland. The Poles had only about a million men under arms. Ironically, England and France had kept Poland from fully mobilizing its army despite the growing threat of war. They feared full Polish mobilization might precipitate German reaction.

Far worse than the difference in the size of the opposing armies was the disparity in their equipment. Germany aimed two thousand warplanes at Poland; the Poles had fewer than one thousand, and most of those were destroyed on the ground by the surprising swiftness of the German attack. Poland had less than a third as many tanks—five hundred to Germany's seventeen hundred. Furthermore, the majority of Polish tanks were World War I vintage, no match for the German panzers.

Yet, even given the surprise of the German attack and the weakness of the Polish army, the swiftness of the German advance shocked the world. Germany had launched a new kind of attack—blitzkrieg, or "lightning war." It seemed that no force could stop it.

While heavy artillery pounded the front, squadrons of devastating Ju-87 Stuka dive-bombers attacked both military and civilian targets behind the Polish lines. Soon Polish roads were clogged with fleeing, panicked civilians dragging a few precious possessions away from the onslaught—the same roads over which the Polish military futilely tried to supply its soldiers.

Meanwhile, attacking armored tanks, armored cars, self-propelled guns, and infantry on motorcycles tore into the Polish defenses and burst into their rear echelons, cutting off pockets of resistance and destroying them at will.

The Poles prayed for rain to bog down the German armor in mud, but the weather continued clear and bright. "Hitler weather," the German soldiers called it. As the Wehrmacht, the German army, advanced across the flat Polish plains, it was obvious within only a few days that the war was lost. All that was uncertain was Hitler's stopping point.

On September 17, Stalin cashed his chip from the secret section of the Soviet-German nonaggression pact signed in August. His troops crossed into Polish territory from the east. There were hardly any Polish soldiers along the eastern border to oppose him. Within a few weeks, he had secured his spoils from the bargain— about one-third of Poland. Germany had swallowed the rest.

The Phony War

France and England, as they had promised Poland, declared war two days after Germany launched its attack. But there was little they could do to relieve Poland's agony. They could only build up their forces in France while they awaited the inevitable German attack. England sent a small force into northern France while most of France's army was concentrated along the Maginot Line, a series of steel and concrete fortifications, pillboxes, and barbed wire entanglements built after World War I specifically to repel a German invasion. It guarded the entire border between France and Germany, from Switzerland to Belgium. Many experts believed it to be impenetrable.

During the 1930s, Germany had constructed its own version, the Siegfried Line. Now the two sides hunkered down behind their respective lines and dared each other to attack. Neither moved during the fall or the winter. In America, safely on the sideline, commentators began calling it the "Phony War."

In April 1940, Hitler moved, but not against France. He sent troops north through hapless Denmark and then into Norway.

Panzers: The Cutting Edge

Germany's single greatest advantage in weaponry at the beginning of the war was the Panzer IV tank. No other country had a tank to match its combination of speed, maneuverability, and firepower. Moreover, the panzer's five-man crews were the best-trained tankmen in the world.

The Panzer IV weighed 20 tons, was 19 feet long, 9 feet wide, and 8 feet high. Across its front, it was protected by armor 1.2 inches thick—enough to withstand most enemy shells—and its sides were covered by still formidable armor just under an inch thick. When traveling on a road, it could reach a speed of 25 miles an hour, outstanding for the time. Even on rugged cross-country terrain, the Panzer IV could move at a 12-mile-an-hour clip. Its huge, 120-gallon gas tanks gave it a range of 125 miles without losing time refueling.

The panzer was armed with a cannon and two machine guns. From the turret, the tank commander could direct the tank's movements to the driver below. Meanwhile, a gunner and loader tended the panzer's 75mm gun. By contrast, the top French tank had a crew of three, with the commander loading, aiming, and firing the gun.

The leading British and French tanks were as well armed as the panzer but could not approach its speed. Not until the Russian T-34s came into wide use in late 1942 did the Allies have a tank to equal the Panzer IV.

The powerful, quick-moving Panzer IV, with its impenetrable armor and tremendous firepower capability, gave Germany a great advantage in weaponry at the beginning of the war.

Stukas: Weapons of Terror

Known as "the Shrieking Vulture," the Stuka dive-bomber terrorized its victims with its screaming engine and deadly bombings.

The Ju-87 Stuka dive-bomber was one of the most effective weapons of the blitzkrieg. Dropping from the sky to deliver a two-thousand-pound bomb with deadly accuracy, it represented a style of attack that had never been seen before.

An ungainly looking craft even by the standards of the day, the Stuka's stubby body, squared-off tail, and fixed landing gear produced a boxy silhouette as it approached its target. But when it nosed over into a vertical power dive, its engine screaming, its broad ailerons wide open on its inverted gull wings, its spat-covered undercarriage resembling talons, the Stuka became a terrifying bird of prey. It was dubbed "the Shrieking Vulture."

That spreading terror was as important as dropping bombs is shown by the fact that many Stukas had sirens mounted under their wings. When they dived on their victims, the unholy scream made everyone on the ground believe a bomb was aimed straight for them.

The plane was a highly effective weapon in the invasions of Poland, the Low Countries, and France. It knocked out bridges, tanks, and other such targets with precision, and its use against civilians helped clog the roads with panicked refugees.

However, the air battles over England showed the Stuka's limitations. Its lack of speed and armament made it an easy target for the faster, more maneuverable British fighters.

The British tried to help the Norwegians, but they were stymied by Germany's superiority in the air. By June, Hitler had secured Norway and its port of Narvik, the main shipping point for Sweden's iron ore. Additionally, Norway's rugged coast provided bases for German submarines with which Hitler planned to cut off England's sea lanes.

In England, Winston Churchill replaced Neville Chamberlain, the British prime minister who two years before had hoped to secure "peace in our time" by appeasing Hitler with the Sudetenland. The new prime minister was a fighter; he epitomized the British bulldog, but he took office with the world crashing around him. He could only offer his countrymen "blood, toil, tears, and sweat."

While most of the world watched Hitler, Stalin was also busy. Having taken its share of Poland, the Soviet Union proceeded to secure its Baltic access by forcing "mutual assistance" pacts on the tiny republics of Estonia, Latvia, and Lithuania. The sham agreements were nothing more than a way to bring the three small countries to heel. In the summer of 1940, they were absorbed into the Soviet Union.

Finland did not knuckle under so easily. Talks aimed at imposing a mutual assistance pact on the Finns broke down. On November 30, 1939, Russian troops marched into Finland. The so-called Winter War turned into an embarrassment for the Russians. Although they were eventually able to force the Finns to cede about a tenth of Finland to the Soviet Union, the cost was much higher than expected. The Finns put up a stout resistance against the badly led Russian army, the result of Stalin's purge of officers a few years before. A peace treaty was not signed until March of 1940. By then, the Soviet Union had revealed unsuspected weakness.

Clad in white as camouflage against the snow, Finnish troops valiantly hold the front line against the Russians.

France Falls

While events were unfolding in Finland, France waited for the German attack. When Germany invaded France in World War I, the world was outraged that it chose to attack through the neutral country of Belgium. Yet, despite that lesson, France pinned its defensive hopes on the Maginot Line, which ended at the Belgian border. On May 10, 1940, the Phony War became real as panzers rolled into Belgium and the Low Countries, Luxembourg, and the Netherlands. Luxembourg surrendered in a day, the Netherlands in five. England and France rushed troops into Belgium but succeeded only in getting them surrounded when the Germans outflanked them all the way to the English Channel.

The desperate Allied army was trapped in the French seaport of Dunkirk, just across the Belgian border. What followed was one of the most remarkable events of the war. From forty miles across the English Channel, a strange armada of Royal Navy destroyers, ferries, fishing boats, pleasure yachts, tugs, even motorboats, set sail, all intent on evacuating the British army. Virtually anything that would float was brought to the rescue. The transports were manned by navy regulars, experienced civilian sailors, and volunteers who had hardly ever been on water. Under heavy shelling by German artillery, 338,000 troops were taken out of Dunkirk. Although they had lost all their tanks and equipment, the army was saved. A disastrous loss had been turned into a kind of victory.

The Allies needed something—anything, even a successful retreat—to lift their spirits. Everywhere else there was disaster. Hitler's end run through Belgium had completely upset French plans to fight a stationary battle along the Maginot Line. On June 5, Hitler launched his blitzkrieg into France. The French army staggered backward. Five days later, Italian dictator Benito Mussolini declared war and invaded France from the south. In the United States, President Franklin D. Roosevelt denounced Mussolini's treachery: "The hand that held the dagger has struck it into the back of its neighbor."

Surrounded by swarms of German soldiers, hundreds of thousands of British troops make a desperate attempt to evacuate the French seaport of Dunkirk.

The Hand That Held the Dagger

Italian dictator Benito Mussolini (1887–1945) achieved power more than a decade before Hitler, and to some extent Hitler modeled his rise on Mussolini's. Eventually, like Hitler, Mussolini led his country down the path of defeat.

In his late teens Mussolini taught school and served in the Italian army. He became a socialist and advanced to a leadership position in the party. In 1909 he went to Austria to work for a socialist newspaper, but he was expelled from that country for advocating revolution. Upon his return to Italy, he continued his socialist activities. Three years later, he became editor of the party's official newspaper. When World War I began, he urged that Italy enter it against Germany, an unpopular position within socialist ranks. He resigned his editorship and founded his own newspaper, *il Popolo d'Italia*, in which he continued to lobby for Italy to go to war. His extreme views brought his expulsion from the Socialist Party. When Italy did indeed enter the war in 1915, he joined the army and was wounded in action.

He declared himself dictator in 1925, and Italy became a totalitarian state with the Fascists controlling the media, police, industry, and education. All other political parties were banned. Foreign observers largely ignored the loss of freedom in Italy, marveling instead at the government's new efficiency. "He made the trains run on time!" was soon a catch-phrase.

Mussolini wanted to acquire colonies to enrich Italy. At the time, Britain had a colonial empire that stretched around the world. France was not far behind. Even such small countries as Belgium and the Netherlands had colonies in Africa and Asia, generating wealth for the home country. Mussolini looked around for an easy conquest. In 1935 his army invaded the African country of Ethiopia. In a contest that pitted spears against tanks and airplanes, the Ethiopians were quickly subdued. Mussolini also supported the Franco side in the Spanish civil war with arms and troops. In 1939 his army attacked and conquered little Albania. Easy victories over weak foes gave him plenty of opportunities to strut and to deliver bombastic speeches, but they also brought him condemnation from the world community. This only strengthened his alliance with Hitler.

When the two dictators first met in the early 1930s, Hitler was profuse in his praise of Mussolini. Apparently, he honestly respected his fellow dictator for having come to power in Italy a decade before the Nazis did in Germany. For his part, the Italian expected their partnership, which was cemented by formal agreement with the Rome-Berlin Axis in 1936, to be one of equals. However, he was caught short by Hitler's attack on Poland and only entered the war with his treacherous invasion of France when that country was all but conquered.

When the Allies invaded Sicily in 1943, Italy rebelled against Fascist rule and surrendered. Mussolini was imprisoned, but Hitler freed him with a daring commando raid. For the remainder of the war, he headed a puppet government under German control in northern Italy. When German resistance collapsed in April of 1945, Mussolini was captured by Italian partisans and murdered. His bullet-riddled body was strung up by the heels in a gas station for all to see.

By June 14 the German army was in Paris. Most French army officers were convinced the war was lost. When Premier Paul Reynaud urged that France fight on, he found himself almost alone in that sentiment. Reynaud resigned, and the new government signed an armistice on June 22. The German blitzkrieg had triumphed again. It had taken Hitler a mere six weeks to conquer France, something Germany could not accomplish in all the four years of World War I.

The Battle of Britain

Hitler was in no particular hurry to defeat England so long as the British would give him a free hand to do as he pleased on the continent. When France fell, he assumed the British would be willing to talk peace.

They were not. Under the inspirational leadership of the pugnacious Churchill, the British fought on alone. Winston Churchill had stirringly addressed the House of Commons on June 4.

A German newsreel photographer films Hitler and his officers in Paris after Germany's successful invasion of France in 1940.

We shall not flag or fail. We shall go on to the end. We shall fight in France, we shall fight on the seas and oceans, we shall fight with growing confidence and growing strength in the air, we shall defend our island, whatever the cost may be, we shall fight on the beaches, we shall fight on the landing grounds, we shall fight in the fields and in the streets, we shall fight in the hills; we shall never surrender.

Hitler's generals made plans to invade England across the Channel, but an invasion was possible only if the German air force, the Luftwaffe, controlled the sky. Hitler chose to believe the boasts of his Luftwaffe commander, Hermann Göring, that the British Royal Air Force, the RAF, could be brought to its knees by his pilots. Beginning in July 1940 he launched raid after raid against RAF bases in what became known as the Battle of Britain.

Although outnumbered, the RAF had skilled and courageous pilots and an excellent fighter, the Spitfire. But, most important, they had radar, which gave them early warning of German attacks. British pilots were already in the air, armed and ready, as the Germans flew across the Channel. They exacted a heavy toll in German aircraft.

Nevertheless, the RAF was on the ropes when the Germans suddenly switched tactics. Believing the exaggerated claims of air victories by their returning pilots, the Germans decided they had defeated the RAF. Instead of continuing to target airfields, in September they began bombing cities. London and other large centers were subjected to vicious bombing raids that had no other purpose than to destroy the morale of the British civilian population. Londoners called it the Blitz, and it went on nearly every night for months as they huddled in underground shelters. But, instead of weakening British will, the Blitz somehow strengthened English determination.

The Germans had also miscalculated the RAF's strength. The Luftwaffe's switch to bombing cities instead of airfields gave the RAF a chance to rebuild, to design and produce new planes and train new pilots. German losses mounted in the skies over England. By May 1941 they had become unbearable. The Blitz ended; the RAF had won. "Never in the field of human conflict," said Churchill at the height of the Blitz, voicing a grateful nation's thanks, "was so much owed by so many to so few."

As workers clean up the debris, the king and queen of England inspect the damage to Buckingham Palace after a Nazi bomb attack.

But though frustrated, Hitler was far from beaten. In fact the Axis was growing. It had begun with a mutual defense pact signed by Germany, Italy, and Japan. Early in 1941 Hitler pressured Bulgaria, Hungary, and Romania into joining. Though less than enthusiastic participants, the three countries had little choice. When the Yugoslav army rebelled and overthrew a puppet government that had agreed to become an Axis member, an enraged Hitler sent in the Wehrmacht and crushed the uprising in eleven days. Nearby Albania got the message and soon joined the Axis.

Having allies had its downside. Mussolini, supposedly Hitler's partner, chafed at what he perceived accurately was his second-class status in the Axis. He set out to do some conquering of his own and overreached himself by invading Greece. When the Greeks seemed likely to defeat the Italians, the German army had to be called in to finish what the Italian dictator had begun.

At this point, England was a mere island off the coast of a continent Hitler controlled from Greece to Norway. It was an annoyance, but it could be left to wither on the vine while his submarines destroyed the ships bringing supplies. No matter what Churchill said, sooner or later England would surrender or starve.

At last Hitler could turn toward his real target—Russia.

Whistling in the Dark

One had only to read *Mein Kampf* to realize that Hitler would eventually turn on Russia. Gaining lebensraum for Germany by confiscating Russian territory had been part of his plan as he rose to power. Stalin thought the attack might come in 1944 or 1945. By then, he was confident, the Soviet Union would be ready.

Hitler, of course, recognized that the longer he waited to attack, the stronger Russia would grow. What if the Soviet Union and England were to join forces sometime down the road? In the summer of 1940, even before the Battle of Britain began, Hitler ordered his generals to draw up plans for the invasion of Russia.

Yet Stalin remained convinced that the German dictator would not attack for several years. He was careful to live up to the letter of the Soviet-German pact, which included provisions that Russia deliver steady supplies of food, oil, and iron ore to Germany. Russians who spoke of a possible war with Germany were officially told to be quiet. A few were even arrested for the "crime" of speculation. Germany was to be given no provocation to even consider war. When one Russian general suggested moving his troops forward to new positions inside the newly conquered Polish territory, he was ordered to remain behind the old Soviet-Polish border. Such an advance might seem provocative to Hitler.

The summer of 1941 arrived with growing rumors of an imminent German attack. Moreover, reports were coming in from Soviet spies confirming the rumors. Unfortunately, other reports said no attack was likely, and Stalin chose to believe those. In mid-June, *Tass*, the Soviet news agency and chief propaganda organ for the Kremlin, took the extraordinary step of announcing flatly that there was no truth to any rumors of an impending attack. After years of communist rule, the ordinary Russian knew better than to take anything *Tass* said at face value, but this pronouncement was so certain, so final, that many felt calmed.

Still, the rumors grew. No amount of Nazi cunning or duplicity could completely mask the huge German army buildup along the Russian border. By June 21 Hitler had 4,200,000 men, 3,500 tanks, 50,000 guns, and 3,900 airplanes aligned against the Soviets. It was the most powerful military force ever assembled. Yet, despite reports that flooded back to Moscow describing the enormous German buildup, Stalin did nothing, apparently believing that any countermove on his part might be regarded as provocative and bring on the very attack he wanted to avoid.

He did not even put his army on alert. The USSR had five million men under arms, but many were poorly trained and many units were poorly led. The war with Finland had shown that. In guns, tanks, and planes, no comparison could be made to German strength. Moreover, the Red Army was badly positioned to withstand a strong attack from the west. More than two million troops were east of Moscow, far from Soviet borders.

On Saturday, June 21, the German ambassador to Moscow, Count Friedrich Werner von der Schulenberg, warned the Russian ambassador to Berlin that the situation had become critical and urged the Soviets to contact Berlin while there was still time. It was a courageous act of conscience, but the Russians interpreted it as an elaborate extortion plot by Hitler to boost supplies of oil and other provisions coming from Russia.

At 3:15 A.M. Sunday morning, June 22, 1941, the commander of Russia's Black Sea fleet telephoned Moscow with news: The port of Sevastopol was being bombed by German airplanes. Even then, the report was not immediately believed, perhaps because Premier Stalin could not be located to tell the others what to think.

Soon reports of bombings of other cities began arriving. By the time Stalin was found, German soldiers were attacking across the border in force. At a 7:00 A.M. meeting with Generals Georgy Zhukov and Semyon Timoshenko, he was informed of the gravity of the situation. Stalin was completely crushed. Turning to the members of the politburo, he said, "All that Lenin created we have lost forever!" He issued a directive ordering the Red Army to repel the invaders and then left the room, not to be seen or heard from for the next several days.

Attack!

To justify this latest cold-blooded example of naked aggression, the Nazi propaganda machine accused the Soviet Union of all sorts of crimes and betrayals: The Russians had failed to deliver the volume

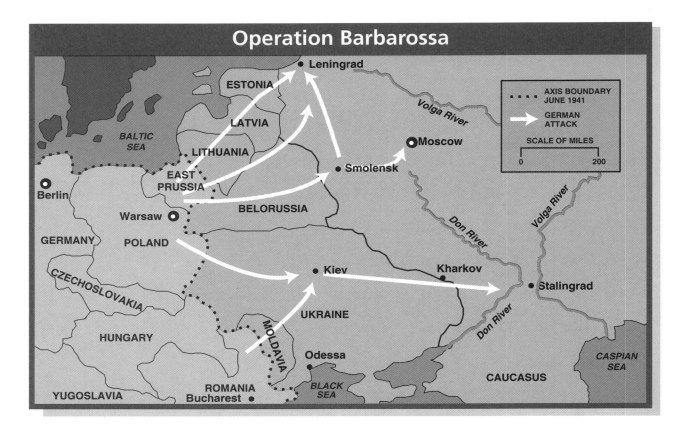

Operation Barbarossa

of supplies they had agreed to in the nonaggression pact; the Soviets were secretly conniving with the British to come into the war against Germany; the USSR had been building an enormous army along its western border in preparation for an attack. It was all nonsense, of course, but nonsense that was believed in Germany, whose citizens had access only to Nazi-controlled news. But they were the only ones Hitler cared to convince.

The invasion of the Soviet Union, code-named Operation Barbarossa, comprised three theaters of operations along a thousand-mile front. To the north, Field Marshal Wilhelm von Leeb's army group, consisting of twenty-one infantry divisions and six armored divisions, tore into the Baltic states of Lithuania, Latvia, and Estonia. Von Leeb's target was Leningrad, an important prize for several reasons. First, Leningrad was the gateway to Russia's northern ports. Secondly, Finland had predictably joined in the attack on Russia and a successful thrust north would allow the Wehrmacht to link up with the Finnish army. And capturing Leningrad was especially important to Hitler for another reason: He was convinced the loss of the city named for the hero of the revolution would crush Russian morale.

At the same time, Field Marshal Fedor von Bock's force— Army Group Center, with thirty infantry divisions and fifteen panzer or motorized divisions—headed straight for the present capital of Moscow 650 miles to the northeast. Most German generals believed the capture of Moscow, Russia's transportation and communication center, was crucial to Barbarossa's success.

Meanwhile, Field Marshal Gerd von Rundstedt's army group of twenty-five infantry, four motorized, four mountain, and five panzer divisions drove east and south. His immediate target was Kharkov, the fourth-largest city and the key to the Ukraine with its wealth of wheat. The Ukraine was the Soviet Union's breadbasket. And beyond the Ukraine lay the Caucasus, rich in the oil Hitler needed to wage mechanized war.

At first all went according to plan. The Russian air force suffered crushing damage. Three hundred planes were shot out of the air; nine hundred were destroyed on the ground. German Stukas had free rein to bomb any city they could reach. The flat terrain lent itself to mechanized war. And the fine weather—"Hitler weather"—held. By the second week in July, all three prongs of the invasion had made excellent progress. Army Group Center was particularly successful, driving four hundred miles into Russia. Almost daily came news that another Russian city had fallen before the Wehrmacht: Novgorod, Brest-Litovsk, Mogilev, Vitebsk, Rostov, Kharkov, Kiev, Kursk, Smolensk, Odessa, Sevastopol. The German generals, many of whom had considered the invasion of Russia a risky proposition, were jubilant. On the eve of the attack, Hitler had confidently predicted, "You have only to kick in the door and the whole rotten structure will come crashing down." Now his prophecy appeared to be coming true.

Soon, Hitler told his generals, they should prepare to disband as many as forty infantry divisions so that the men could be put to work in factories. In the meantime, he ordered that troops and supplies be withdrawn from the most successful thrust, Army Group Center, and distributed to the northern and southern prongs. His generals, certain that Moscow was the most important

Members of the Red Army fend off German attackers in an effort to retain what is left of their mostly demolished city.

goal, attempted to dissuade him from weakening the assault but Hitler was riding a crest of infallibility. The generals' protests were weak and went unheeded. Few would argue to Hitler's face. In placing the capture of Leningrad and the Ukraine above that of Moscow, Hitler was putting political considerations ahead of military logic. Leningrad was important to him because of its propaganda value; the Ukraine would yield food and manufacturing booty to send back to the Fatherland. And deeper into the Ukraine lay Stalingrad—another city with a symbolically loaded name.

Russia Resists

In the first days of Operation Barbarossa, German soldiers were often surprised and delighted to be greeted not as invaders but as liberators. This was most common in the Ukraine, and for good reason. Until 1939 the western Ukraine had been part of Poland. The Soviet Union had acquired it as part of its pact with Germany, and the USSR was generally detested by the populace. The eastern Ukraine had suffered grievously under the collectivization of the 1930s and had no love for Stalin, Moscow, or communism. Upon entering villages, German soldiers were likely to find themselves bedecked with flowers while banners welcomed them as bringers of freedom.

The elation lasted only a few days. Then the S.S. arrived. Had the Germans treated the Russian people with a minimum of human decency, millions might have risen against Stalin and the communists. Instead, the actions of the S.S. drove the population to embrace Stalin.

Early in March 1941, more than three months before the invasion, Hitler had issued what came to be called his Commissar Order. The commissars were political officers attached to army units; they shared responsibility with the military commanders and indoctrinated the troops with communist dogma. Hitler ordered that the "bearers of ideologies directly opposed to National Socialism" be "liquidated." He further declared that any German soldiers who broke international law—by shooting prisoners, for example—were "excused." Soldiers on all sides violated international law during the course of the war, but it was the S.S. that set the standard for brutal, inhuman atrocities.

Their mandate was to murder political commissars, but with Hitler's blessing they defined "commissar" in its widest possible interpretation. This included anyone expressing a political opinion. Or an anti-Nazi sentiment. Or anyone suspected of hindering the German offensive in any way. Or any Jew.

When a transmitter was damaged in Kiev and the saboteur could not be discovered, four hundred men were chosen at random and shot. On another occasion, more than two hundred prisoners were taken from a jail, led to a drainage ditch, and killed. The ditch was not quite filled, so another eighty prisoners were led out and slaughtered. Ironically, thirty of these were volunteer workers—Nazi sympathizers—from another part of the country who were being boarded at the jail until suitable lodging could be found. Men, women, and children were murdered for no other reason than they happened to be available to die. One group of five hundred S.S. claimed responsibility for ninety thousand deaths.

Hitler's barbaric S.S. went on a brutal rampage in the Ukraine, killing and torturing thousands of soldiers and citizens. Here, workers prepare a mass grave for the bodies of forty-six Russian soldiers who were gunned down by Hitler's men.

Behind the barbarity was a cold-blooded purpose. Hitler planned to fill the Ukraine, his much-coveted lebensraum, with German settlers after the war. The first step was to get rid of the native population. Outright murder was one method. The Nazis also destroyed sanitation facilities and withheld medical treatment so that disease could take a greater toll. Thousands of peasants were shipped west to work as slave laborers in factories or to meet their ultimate fate in concentration camps. No one knows how many Ukrainians were murdered in one way or another. Some estimate the number of Russian civilian deaths, including those attributed to starvation and disease, at twenty million. At the end of the war, what once had been thriving villages were left with only a few old men. Some villages disappeared altogether.

But while such barbarity suited Hitler's master plan for his master race, it was counterproductive in that it gave rise to a growing guerrilla resistance. German soldiers soon found stones instead of flowers being hurled at them. Small acts of sabotage disrupted communications and delayed the arrival of supplies. Soldiers alone and in small groups were sometimes ambushed. Such tactics could not turn the tide of the German offensive, but they could slow it.

On October 8, Hitler's press chief announced, "For all military purposes Soviet Russia is done with." By then, however, most German soldiers on the front knew that to be untrue.

For eleven days after the initial German attack, Stalin was unseen and unheard by the Russian people. Rumors abounded that he was mad with anger, paralyzed by shock, lost in depression, dead drunk—or simply dead. Then, on July 3, he spoke to the people over the radio. His speech was perhaps the strangest of his career. In a soft, halting voice, he opened by addressing his "sisters, brothers, friends." He reminded his people of how their ancestors had defeated the invasion by Napoléon in 1812 and asked them to resist the Nazis with the same vigor. He went on to outline the German invasion as an attempt "to seize our lands watered by the sweat of our brows, to seize the grain and oil secured by the labor of our hands." Several times he paused and listeners could hear him shuffle papers or drink some water. Stalin talked of "a war for the freedom of our Motherland." Every Russian citizen had been personally attacked and had everything to lose in this "patriotic war."

Soldiers must stand and fight for their homes and their loved ones, Stalin went on. And when retreat was necessary, the people must "scorch the earth" first.

> The enemy must not be left a single engine, a single railway car, a single pound of grain, a single gallon of fuel. All valuable property that cannot be withdrawn must be destroyed. . . . Blow up bridges and roads, set fire to forests, stores and transport.

The Wehrmacht continued to advance through the summer, but its pace slowed. And most of what was captured had been rendered worthless by partisan torches.

The very shape of the three-pronged German attack dictated a slowdown. In effect, the German armies streamed through narrow points of entry and necessarily slowed as they fanned outward. As the Wehrmacht simultaneously drove north, east, and south, the front line grew longer and correspondingly thinner. Troops had to be spread over ever-widening arcs and weak spots appeared. Reserves were called up to fill gaps, but they were not the battle-hardened veterans who had begun the attack. In many cases they were units sent by other Axis partners such as Italy, Hungary, or Romania, soldiers who were not so well trained or equipped as the Wehrmacht. And every mile advanced added another mile to the German supply lines.

After the first shock, the Red Army gave ground grudgingly. Stalin had ordered, "Hold; if necessary, die!" At the same time Hitler was declaring victory, German generals in the field were remarking on the determination shown by their enemy. "The conduct of the Russian troops," wrote one general, ". . . was in striking contrast to the behavior of the Poles and Western Allies in defeat. Even when encircled the Russians stood their ground and fought."

Even more disheartening to the Germans was the apparently endless supply of troops and equipment the Russians could throw into battle. Before launching the invasion, Chief of the General Staff Franz Halder wrote in his diary, they had estimated the size of the Red Army at 200 divisions. By August the Germans had identified 360 Russian divisions, and who knew how

Thousands of Russian soldiers heeded Stalin's call to fight the Germans. The Russians shocked the Germans by dispatching a seemingly endless supply of troops and refusing to surrender easily.

many more might be available? Von Rundstedt, so confident before the invasion, insisted later, "I realized soon after the attack was begun that everything that had been written about Russia was nonsense."

In September, Kiev, the capital of the Ukraine, fell. Hitler called it "the greatest battle in the history of the world." Indeed, it was a punishing blow to the Soviet Union. The Germans claimed to have taken 665,000 prisoners, 3,718 guns, and 886 tanks. Strategically, however, Kiev was just another spot on the seemingly endless road into the Ukraine. It had been captured only with the help of General Heinz Guderian's tanks, pulled at Hitler's order from the assault on Moscow. The Germans were still advancing but they faced a deadline. When the fearsome Russian winter arrived, everything would grind to a halt.

Despite the victories in the south, the precious oil fields still lay far to the southeast beyond the Caucasus Mountains. To the north, Leningrad was placed under a terrible siege, but it refused to surrender.

Shortly after Japan's December 1941 attack at Pearl Harbor, Hitler declared war on the United States.

In October, von Bock's Army Group Center drove to within forty miles of Moscow. Von Bock himself, riding with an advance party, was at one point only ten miles from the city. Far in the distance, he could see sun glinting off the turrets of the Kremlin. He would get no closer. The fall rains began, miring his tanks in mud. Then the Red Army mustered a surprise counterattack far stronger than the Germans had believed possible. Army Group Center was pushed back from Moscow, the first retreat of any consequence for Hitler's Wehrmacht. As the December snows began to fall, von Bock asked for permission to put his army into defensive positions. Reluctantly, and only after much coaxing, Hitler agreed.

Operation Barbarossa had engulfed a huge chunk of Soviet territory, inflicted massive casualties on the Red Army, and destroyed tons of Russian armament. At first glance, it seemed like a great success.

In reality, it had failed. Its major objectives had not been reached. Moscow, Leningrad, and the oil fields all remained in Russian hands. The Wehrmacht's casualties, though not nearly so great as the Red Army's, were nevertheless potentially more crippling. Germany did not have the bottomless well of manpower available to the Soviet Union nor could equipment be so readily replaced. If nothing else, the counterattacks mounted in the fall proved that the Russian bear still had a lot of fight left. All Hitler could do was wait out the winter and renew the attack in the spring.

On December 7, 1941, Japan launched a surprise attack on the United States at Pearl Harbor. Axis Japan was part of the tripartite pact with Italy and Germany, but since the Japanese had begun the fight, Germany was not obligated to join in its war against the United States. Nevertheless, Hitler declared war on America four days after the Pearl Harbor attack.

CHAPTER THREE

Operation Blau

Compared with the grandiose, three-pronged attack of Operation Barbarossa in 1941, the German offensive of 1942—called Operation Blau (Blue)—had much more modest aims. Instead of three simultaneous attacks all along the Russian front, Blau put all its military eggs into one territorial basket. Troops still faced Moscow and the siege of Leningrad continued, but the offensive thrust was to the south. Hitler, the master strategist, at least in his own mind, had decided the Caucasus oil fields had to be taken.

Even Hitler by now realized that Germany could not sustain three major offensives at once. During Barbarossa, Germany's losses in men and machines all along the front had been greater than anticipated against the tenacious Red Army. Russian losses had been higher than those of Germany, of course, but the Soviet Union's huge population could absorb such losses and churn out replacements. In a war of attrition, Germany was outmanned.

The bitter Russian winter of 1941–1942 took its toll on the German invaders. The plan had been for a quick defeat of the Soviet Union similar to the fates that befell Poland and France. In the rosiest scenario, the Russian people would have rebelled against Stalin and their communist rulers, in effect turning the whole country over to Germany. That proved a pipe dream, but even well into the fall of 1941, the Germans expected to be comfortably in Moscow and Leningrad by the time winter arrived. Instead, the stout Russian defense and counterattack left the Wehrmacht to spend the winter hunkered down on the Russian plains. That was the last thing Hitler expected. Unprepared, many soldiers faced cold and snow still wearing their summer uniforms. Coats, boots, and fuel were promised but seldom provided. Soldiers froze to death at their posts and sickness was rampant.

The combination of winter hardships and the losses of 1941 meant the Wehrmacht was much weaker by the spring of 1942 than it had been a year earlier. And throughout the winter the Soviets had been catching up to the Germans in armament production. Whole factories had been uprooted from the German path of conquest and moved to safety behind the Ural Mountains to the east. In the long run, the Soviets had the raw materials and the manufacturing ability to outproduce their enemy.

Significantly, the quality of Soviet armament was on the rise, too. Once the United States entered the war, it began shipping tons of equipment to its new Soviet allies. But Russia's own manufacturing also improved steadily. The new T-34 tanks produced in Russian factories were a match for German panzers. At the beginning of the war, the Russians actually had more tanks than the Wehrmacht—that is, on the books. Unfortunately, only a small percentage were of much use. The rest were obsolete, inadequately armored, or out of commission with a variety of maintenance ills. By late 1941 a crash building effort had the T-34s rolling into action, some so new they had not even been painted. It was said that often the tank crew helped put the finishing touches on a tank and then drove it right off the assembly line. As assembly methods became more efficient, the time it took to produce a single tank was reduced from 110 hours to 40.

Given the Soviets' ability to outproduce the Germans and Russia's seemingly endless reservoir of manpower, Operation Blau, aimed at the Caucasus oil fields, made good sense. Without oil, a tank became just another standing pillbox. Without oil, the regenerated Russian air force was grounded. Without oil, heavy

Hoping to cripple the Russian troops by cutting off their supply of oil, the Nazis focused their attack on the Caucasus oil fields.

artillery could not be moved. Without oil, mechanized warfare ground to a halt. Germany could win only by moving faster and with more punch than the Soviets. Hitler confidently expected Operation Blau to regain the initiative for his army.

Perhaps, Hitler dreamed, even more might be accomplished. If all went perfectly, Operation Blau would capture the Caucasus oil fields and then roll on through Iran and link up with General Erwin Rommel's Afrika Corps at the Suez Canal. Rommel was at that time wreaking havoc across North Africa and seemed certain to wrest Egypt from the British. If Blau could reach Rommel, the Mediterranean would be turned into a German lake. Britain's lifeline to India would be severed. Surely such a triumph would cause even the intransigent Churchill to seek peace.

Both sides waited for the spring mud to dry and make the roads passable. Both sides looked ahead to great victories.

The Kharkov Debacle

Stalin's dreams were not as all-encompassing as Hitler's, but he thought he saw a way to deal the Germans a major blow. Unfortunately, his plans were based on two misconceptions. First, he was certain the Germans would aim their main attack at Moscow. Second, the success of the late counterattack of 1941 convinced him that the Red Army was ready to defeat the Wehrmacht in open battle. As a result, he prematurely concentrated the bulk of his forces around Moscow and prepared to launch a surprise attack. Gathering his top military advisers around him, he called for suggestions.

General Georgy Zhukov, the man who had planned the successful counterattack of the previous winter, proposed a limited offensive to the west of Moscow. The rest of the Red Army would remain on the defensive while it built up its strength. Stalin angrily rejected Zhukov's "half measures." He wanted a major offensive.

The final plan approved by Stalin called for more than a half million men and over a thousand tanks to smash into the German lines from the southwest. The target was Kharkov, Russia's fourth-largest city, captured by the Germans the previous year. Zhukov continued to have strong doubts.

Nikita Khrushchev (right), who would later rise in rank and lead the Soviet Union, commanded the army unit that launched the 1942 counterattack against the Germans at Kharkov.

Zhukov

At the beginning of the war, many Red Army officers were incompetent, owing their rank to Communist Party politics rather than to ability. A notable exception was Georgy Zhukov. By the end of the war he had become the one Russian general who could be considered the equal of Eisenhower, MacArthur, and Montgomery among Allied commanders. Equally brilliant at a strategic planning table or leading his men in the field, Zhukov combined stunning ability and a cold-blooded pragmatism.

The general was in his early forties when Hitler invaded the Soviet Union. Zhukov reorganized the defense of Leningrad, keeping the city from being overrun. Soon after that he found himself facing the seemingly impossible task of turning back the all-conquering Wehrmacht at the gates of Moscow. When a nervous Stalin asked him if Moscow could be saved, he answered confidently that it would be if Stalin would give him the men he needed. The dictator scraped up the manpower and Zhukov delivered the victory, the first of any consequence for the USSR.

As the war progressed, Stalin took bows as a great military leader, but in fact he relied more and more heavily on Zhukov to make military decisions. He promoted him to field marshal, the highest rank in the Soviet army, but, ever suspicious, he refused to place him in charge of the entire army. After Zhukov had orchestrated the Russian victory in the east and the war was over, Stalin assigned him to only minor posts because he feared that Zhukov's popularity might make him a rival.

With Stalin's death in 1953, Zhukov's star rose again, and he became defense minister two years later. He helped Nikita Khrushchev achieve power, but again his popularity and ability were perceived as a threat. Khrushchev had him removed from the Politburo in 1957. Zhukov died in 1974.

On May 12, 1942, the offensive began under the command of General Semyon Timoshenko, with Nikita Khrushchev as political commissar. In the unique Soviet system, command of an army unit was divided between a military officer and a Communist Party officer. Khrushchev would eventually rise to the leadership of the Soviet Union, but in 1942 he found himself at a crossroads. If the offensive succeeded, his star would rise; if it failed, he fully expected Stalin to lay the blame on him.

For five days, all went well. Stalin crowed to his generals; his daring strategy had been right! Timoshenko's force drove to within twelve miles of Kharkov, seventy miles into German-held territory. There was little opposition—too little. Khrushchev and Timoshenko sensed a trap and called a halt to the advance in order to take up defensive positions. Then word came from Stalin: The offensive was to continue. Desperately, Khrushchev telephoned

Stalin to plead for new orders. Stalin would not come to the phone. Instead Khrushchev's plea was relayed through Georgy Malenkov, an old political rival of Khrushchev's. Not surprisingly, Stalin's orders remained unchanged.

But Khrushchev was right. The Red Army had walked into a trap. By coincidence, the offensive had been launched into the very area where the Wehrmacht, preparing for Operation Blau, was at its greatest strength. Taken by surprise, the Germans simply fell back and off to the sides while the Russians drove blindly ahead.

On May 18, von Bock, in overall command of the area, launched a counterattack into the Soviet flank from the north. The next day, Lieutenant General Friedrich Paulus's armor tore into the flank from the south. Most of the Russian force was caught in a giant pincers. When von Bock's and Paulus's men closed the pincers, the Russian Fifty-seventh Army, Sixth Army, and part of the Ninth Army were trapped. More than two hundred thousand Soviet soldiers surrendered in the disaster. When Hitler received word, he exulted, "The Russian is dead!"

Stalin did not put the blame for the disaster on Khrushchev, at least not publicly. Privately, he mentioned to him that during World War I, officers losing major battles were often shot. Khrushchev decided that the only thing that saved him from a bullet was that there were too many witnesses to his begging Stalin to allow a retreat.

Blau Begins

The Russian offensive pushed back the start of Operation Blau. Hitler delayed it further by sending contingents of von Bock's army group on minor sorties. As a consequence nearly all of June had passed before Blau could be mounted.

On June 28, von Bock sent two of his three armies—the Fourth Panzer Army and the Second Army—exploding out of the Kursk area north of Kharkov. They drove east, heading for the city of Voronezh one hundred miles away on the Don River.

The Don, one of the two great waterways of southern Russia, begins south of Moscow and flows in a generally southeastern direction past Voronezh for another 250 miles until it comes to within 50 miles of Stalingrad, located on the Volga River, Russia's second great waterway. The Volga begins north of Moscow, flows far to the east, then swings back on a southwesterly course. After nearly joining, the two great rivers turn in opposite directions, the Don going southwest to empty into the Sea of Azov and on into the Black Sea. Meanwhile, just below Stalingrad, the Volga veers southeast and flows to the Caspian Sea.

According to Operation Blau, von Bock was to take Voronezh, then roar down the Don to where it bent away from the Volga. At that point, he would seal off Stalingrad, giving him control of both rivers, cutting off Moscow from the south, and protecting the flank of the force driving south into the Caucasus to take the oil fields.

Two days after von Bock headed for Voronezh, the Sixth Army under Lieutenant General Paulus left Kharkov and smashed northeast toward the same city. The Germans planned to catch the bulk of Russian defenders between von Bock and Paulus. Surprisingly, they met virtually no resistance and took very few prisoners. Something was wrong.

"The Russians," wrote a German war correspondent, "who up to this time had fought stubbornly over each kilometer withdrew without firing a shot. It was quite disquieting to plunge into this vast area without finding a trace of the enemy."

A Change in Tactics

The Russians had indeed changed their tactics. Stalin—no doubt on the advice of Zhukov—had ordered Timoshenko to fall back and let the Germans use up their supplies against empty space. The stand would be made at Stalingrad. But at that moment Stalingrad was desperately unready to fight off the German onslaught. More than anything else, the Soviets needed time to prepare. Fortunately, the Germans gave them just that.

Hitler was angry. Although von Bock and Paulus were gobbling up landscape, they were not taking huge numbers of prisoners as anticipated. On July 3 he flew to von Bock's headquarters and began dismantling the carefully crafted Operation Blau. His instructions to von Bock were now that the general had the option of bypassing Voronezh if he liked. He could instead wheel and drive down the Don and then cross over to attack Stalingrad. "I no longer insist on the capture of the town, Bock," he said. "Nor, indeed, do I consider it necessary. You are free, if you wish, to drive southward at once."

The Germans' careful planning was giving way to Hitler's spur-of-the-moment inspirations—a sure recipe for disaster. Orders were hastily ad-libbed. One commander, meeting no resistance on his way to Voronezh, had earlier requested permission to break off and head cross-country. His request was turned down. Then, suddenly, he was ordered to drive to the Don as he had asked. But, within a few hours, those orders were countermanded and he was directed back toward Voronezh.

Meanwhile von Bock learned that some of his units were already within two miles of Voronezh and poised to enter the city. As far as he was concerned, bypassing the city was no longer an option. He attacked in force, expecting to roll right through in no time at all. However, resistance was stronger than he had anticipated. Stalin, mistakenly believing that the Germans intended to turn north for Moscow three hundred miles away, ordered reinforcements into Voronezh. Even when von Bock detached some units to head down the Don, the Russians at Voronezh fought fiercely to buy time for Stalingrad. It took ten days to secure the town—ten precious days that the Soviets at Stalingrad used to build defenses.

Von Bock was finally able to disengage from Voronezh and turn his main force toward Stalingrad by mid-July. But by then his tanks were running low on fuel and ammunition. More delay.

And then Hitler made a disastrous decision. With Blau's timetable abandoned, he was impatient to reach the Caucasus. He ordered von Bock's force split in half. Army Group A, consisting of the Seventeenth Army and the First Panzer Army, was handed over to General Wilhelm List with orders to drive south toward Rostov. From there, List was to complete the capture of the Caucasus begun the year before in Operation Barbarossa and then go on to capture the oil fields. As if that were not enough on his plate, List was also ordered to take over the entire north shore of the Black Sea. Von Bock, with the remainder of his force (now called Army Group B) was left the job of racing for the Volga to Stalingrad, thereby securing Army Group A's flank. He protested vigorously, pointing out that because it had much farther to travel than Army Group B, List's Army Group A would be taking more than half his supplies, leaving him desperately short. Hitler's answer was to fire von Bock. The honor of capturing—not merely sealing off—Stalingrad with less than half of the original force was handed to General Maximilian von Weichs.

Splitting one's force was a classic error to a veteran general like von Bock. But the force was not only split in two; the two parts were diverging at a right angle, Army Group A going south and Army Group B heading east. That opened a dangerous gap between them that could only grow wider the farther they advanced. Furthermore, supplying two separate forces was obviously more difficult than supplying one, especially when both groups were moving farther away from the supply sources back in Germany. "There is no alternative but to face the fact that I have been made a monstrous scapegoat," von Bock wrote.

Army Group A

Hitler, however, was convinced that Russia was already as good as defeated and that he needed only energetic officers to complete the task. He immediately compounded List's problems by stripping Army Group A of nine divisions. Two divisions of motorized infantry were sent to France because Hitler feared the British might launch an invasion across the English Channel. Two panzer divisions were sent back to Army Group Center to line up opposite Moscow. Five divisions were sent far north to take part in the "final" assault on Leningrad. The subjugation of Leningrad would remain an unrealized dream for Hitler.

At first, his confidence that List's Army Group A would have little trouble in the south appeared justified. List's troops drove

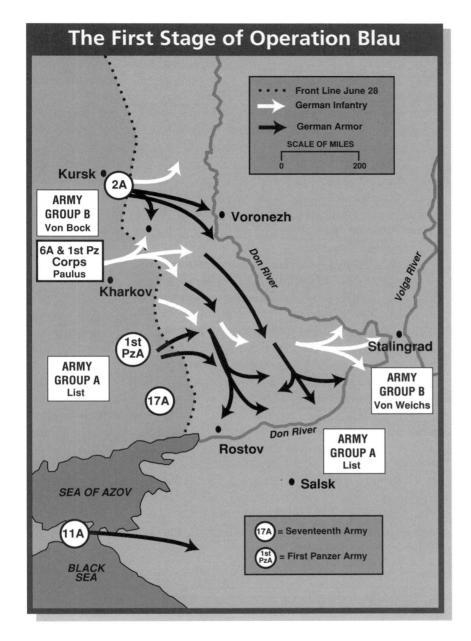

The First Stage of Operation Blau

Front Line June 28
German Infantry
German Armor
SCALE OF MILES
0   200

Kursk
2A
ARMY GROUP B
Von Bock
Voronezh
6A & 1st Pz
Corps
Paulus
Don River
Volga River
Kharkov
1st PzA
ARMY GROUP A
List
17A
Stalingrad
ARMY GROUP B
Von Weichs
Don River
Rostov
ARMY GROUP A
List
SEA OF AZOV
Salsk
11A
BLACK SEA

17A = Seventeenth Army
1st PzA = First Panzer Army

quickly to the gates of Rostov, at the mouth of the Don where it empties into the Sea of Azov. The city was defended fanatically by the Russians, however, and for the first time the Wehrmacht found itself involved in vicious street fighting. The German advantage in mechanization was nullified as the Russians barricaded streets, waited in ambush in cellars, sniped from rooftops, and threw Molotov cocktails. These homemade hand grenades, named after the Soviet foreign minister, Vyacheslav Molotov, were bottles of gasoline with fuses. When the bottles were thrown against a target such as a tank or an advancing infantryman, they exploded, sending flaming gas in all directions.

Even when their position was hopeless, few Russians were willing to surrender. The Germans soon learned that an apparently dead Russian could not be blandly bypassed; he was likely to suddenly spring to his feet behind them and begin firing a machine gun. For several days the fighting was intense, but despite everything the defenders could do, List's troops were able to subdue Rostov by the end of July and move into the Caucasus.

The magnitude of the task they were undertaking is made obvious by a glance at a map. The nearest oil field at Voroshilovak was well over a hundred miles to the south. Baku, the most distant of the oil fields, was seven hundred miles from Rostov, farther than the distance from the Soviet border to Rostov. And to reach Baku, the Germans would have to cross the towering Caucasus Mountains.

Each step Army Group A took into the Caucasus lengthened its supply lines. The irony was that List was soon in dire need of fuel even as he was advancing into some of the world's richest oil fields. The Russians, of course, rendered those fields useless to the Wehrmacht by setting fire to the wells and wrecking the equipment. Fuel was flown and trucked in from Romania, but the distance was so great that the planes and trucks used up as much fuel as they brought in. Eventually, to save fuel, the Germans obtained camels to bring in their oil. The camels, of course, used no oil, but they were much slower than mechanized transport.

Nevertheless, List continued to advance against comparatively light resistance through most of August. Then, just as his fuel needs became critical, Russian defenses stiffened. The offensive slowed to a crawl and it became obvious that the more distant oil fields would not be taken in 1942. Some of List's troops were able to reach the Caucasus Mountains and scale 18,510-foot-high Mount Elbrus, the range's highest peak, but the feat had more publicity value than strategic advantage.

In the meantime, Army Group A's position was precarious. Its long, thinly guarded left flank was exposed to a Soviet counterattack from the east. Hitler doubted the Soviets could mount a counterattack at that time; his generals were not so sure. At any rate, the longer List's flank remained exposed, the more risky was his position in light of increasing Soviet strength.

The key to the situation was Stalingrad.

City on the Spot

Stalingrad, with a population of a half million, was the Soviet Union's third-largest industrial city, an important manufacturing and rail center. Fully one-quarter of Russia's tanks and mechanized vehicles were built there. For that reason alone, it made an inviting target for the Wehrmacht. Yet, surprisingly, the original plan for Operation Blau called for the city to be sealed off from the west rather than captured. But as the summer of 1942 wore on, the Germans realized that Stalingrad was far more important for reasons other than its factories.

The city is a thirty-mile-long ribbon along the west bank of the Volga at that river's westernmost bend. It was a dagger pointed at the flank of List's Army Group A. It could be supplied by water from the north or southwest, to say nothing of its own manufacturing capabilities. If the Soviets were to menace Army Group A, the attack would surely come out of Stalingrad. So long as the city was in Russian hands, the German gains of the summer were at risk. On the other hand, once the Germans captured the city, they would be in position to pivot north and threaten Moscow.

The Gate to the North

Stalingrad was also the gate to the north through which flowed the precious oil from the southern fields. If the Germans could not capture those fields, then depriving the Soviets of their oil was the next best thing. Taking Stalingrad would cut the Soviet Union in two.

Hitler, of course, had another reason for wanting Stalingrad. To him, its symbolic importance was uppermost. He was convinced that losing the city named for the Russian dictator would be a crushing blow to Soviet morale. The destruction of the city became an obsession with him. Eventually, decisions based on his emotions would doom his army at Stalingrad and, ultimately, his Third Reich.

After the war, both Soviet and German historians agreed that the city could have been taken with relative ease at the end of July. Its defenses were weak in part because Stalin continued to hold reserves around Moscow in the belief that the Russian capital was Germany's goal. Had Paulus's panzers raced down the Don River from Voronezh and then cut across the forty-mile strip from the Don to the Volga and Stalingrad, history would have been changed.

However, the assault on Stalingrad was delayed, first by the splitting of von Bock's force into Army Groups A and B and the necessary division of supplies. Paulus's armor, which was to lead the charge, waited eighteen days until its fuel supplies could be replenished. Once under way, Paulus's Sixth Army moved smartly down the Don and won a great victory at Kalach, trapping more than seventy thousand Soviet troops. The road was clear to Stalingrad, but Paulus spent two more weeks clearing out pockets of resistance at Kalach. And while he dawdled, forty miles east the defenders of Stalingrad worked night and day to turn the city into a fortress.

Although von Weichs was nominally in charge of the attack on Stalingrad, Hitler preferred to deal directly with the generals at the front. Von Weichs faded into the background while Friedrich Paulus, leading the offensive, became Hitler's "man." The fifty-two-year-old Paulus was a favorite of Hitler's. Most of Hitler's generals came from the old Prussian aristocracy and Hitler could never forgive them their ingrained sense of superiority. He always believed they were looking down their noses at him. Paulus, however, was comfortably middle class like Hitler himself. Nor did it hurt their relationship that Paulus openly admired Hitler's military judgment.

The tall, thin Paulus had his oddities. Extremely fastidious, he bathed and changed his uniform twice a day and always wore gloves to avoid dirt. Some fellow officers sarcastically called him "Our Most Elegant Gentleman." At his best as a staff officer planning operations—he had been one of the architects of Barbarossa—he was slow and meticulous in the field. According to some, these traits disguised a lack of decisiveness. On August 21, he was at last ready to make his lunge on Stalingrad. Under his command he had 250,000 men, 500 tanks, and 7,000 guns and mortars. He saw no reason to rush across the forty miles between Kalach and Stalingrad. The advance over the plain resembled a stroll more than an attack. After all, he fully expected to take the city in a day.

Missed Opportunities

On the morning of August 23, Lieutenant General Hans Hube's 16th Panzer Division, ranging far ahead of the Sixth Army's main body, approached the northern outskirts of the city. Hube, who had lost his left arm in World War I, was a respected fighter. His troops called him "the Man." Suddenly, Hube's tanks came under artillery fire, but the shelling was wildly inaccurate. One by one, the panzers efficiently destroyed thirty-seven Russian guns. When the Germans investigated their handiwork, they were surprised to see that the artillery had been manned by Russian women factory workers.

Hube quickly rolled through the Stalingrad suburb of Rynok all the way to the bank of the Volga. To many of his soldiers, the quickness of the advance brought back memories of the glorious blitzkrieg days in Poland. That night, Hube's men had a ringside seat to the heaviest Luftwaffe raid in over a year. The Germans threw every available airplane against the city, even to the extent of tossing incendiary bombs from transports. By dawn most of the city had been leveled or was in flames. An estimated forty thousand Russians were dead. The Luftwaffe commander, General Wolfram von Richthofen, cousin of the famous "Red Baron" flying ace of World War I, wrote confidently in his diary, "We simply paralyzed the Russians."

But Hube soon discovered such was not the case. He sent his panzers against the huge north-end tractor factory where

tanks were built but was stopped within a half mile of his goal by unexpected resistance. Somehow during the night, while bombs fell from the air, the Russians had managed to create a strong line of defense along a nearby hill. Mixed in with units from the Sixty-second Army were militiamen, women factory workers, and literally anyone capable of carrying a gun. Unpainted tanks rolled off the assembly line and right into battle.

The next day, Hube renewed his attack but was again repulsed. Meanwhile, Russian army units had filtered in behind him and the majority of Paulus's armor had not yet arrived. Hube's position was becoming perilous. He was surrounded and his fuel and ammunition were running low. His logical move would have been to break out to the west and link up with Paulus, but Hitler had given orders that "The 16th Panzer will hold its positions in all circumstances." Hube had no choice but to hunker down in Rynok and hope Paulus arrived before it was too late.

The Russians had stalled Hube, but to the south another threat loomed. General Hermann "Papa" Hoth's Fourth Panzer Army had at first been sent south as part of List's drive on the Caucasus, then recalled and directed northeast toward Stalingrad. On September 9, impatient with List's progress, Hitler fired him. By August 20, the Fourth Panzer was about twenty-five miles

Russian women played an important role in the Battle of Stalingrad. In addition to caring for the wounded and working in factories to produce war matériel, they engaged in combat when needed. Here, a group of women carry gas decontamination equipment that will be used in case of a German attack.

south of the city, stalled by the Soviet Sixty-fourth Army entrenched behind a heavily fortified line of hills. Hoth hammered at the Russians for a week, taking heavy losses for little gain. Frustrated, Hoth rethought his problem. The hilly, ravine-pocked terrain put his tanks at a disadvantage. Clearly the solution was to fight his battle on more tank-friendly ground. Secretly, he pulled his tanks out of the battle line and reassembled them thirty miles to the southwest. To conceal his maneuver, he moved his infantry into the abandoned tank positions. On August 29 he launched his armor north, outflanking the hills and roaring on toward Stalingrad.

The Russians were stunned. Hoth's brilliant move offered an extraordinary opportunity. If Paulus drove south immediately and linked with Hoth, the bulk of the Soviet defenders would be cut off and surrounded on the plain to the west of Stalingrad, leaving the weakened city to be taken easily. But the indecisive Paulus was not an officer who could adapt well to sudden changes along the battlefront. While Hoth waited, Paulus worried about exposing his left flank to attacks from the north. The link between Paulus and Hoth was not completed for three days. By then most of the Russian army had retreated safely into the city.

Stalingrad would have to be taken in house-to-house fighting.

The War of the Rats

The defenders of Stalingrad, the Sixty-second Army, had been badly battered. By early September it had perhaps fifty thousand men and one hundred tanks deployed within the city in an area about twenty miles long and a few miles wide. Against them Paulus hurled one hundred thousand men and five hundred tanks, as well as a thousand airplanes. On the face of it, the Russians were doomed.

However, the Germans' greatest strength was their ability to maneuver their armor in open terrain, an advantage lost in the close confines of street-to-street warfare. Nor was control of the air of much value in a firefight whose opponents might be only yards apart. Not even the German superiority in numbers was an overwhelming advantage in a battle where a few barricaded men with machine guns could hold off platoons of advancing infantry. Once the fighting moved into Stalingrad itself, it often became much like the trench battles of World War I, in which foot soldiers were sent against fortified positions. Instead of trenches, the Russians used the rubble of their destroyed city to defend every foot. The Germans had to explore every destroyed building for fear that a machine gunner might be lurking behind a pile of bricks. As often as not, that was the case. If a building remained standing, the fighting was often room-to-room from cellar to attic.

One German survivor described how his unit would spend a whole day clearing a street, slowly, one house at a time. Then the next morning they would discover a Russian machine gun firing away at their rear. It took the Germans a while to discover the Russian trick. The buildings were built one against another. During the night the Soviets would knock holes through the attic walls and then scurry across the rafters to set up their machine gun behind their enemy. The German soldiers called it "the war of the rats."

A City No More

At the beginning of the battle, the city had a half million civilian inhabitants. Thousands fled across the Volga but the Luftwaffe kept the river under constant attack and an appalling number died. Many more civilians kept working, producing the weapons used to defend the city. Through September, despite heavy bombing and shelling, the tractor factory produced two hundred tanks. Other civilians took up arms and fought beside the soldiers of the Sixty-second Army. When the Battle of Stalingrad finally ended five months later, only 1,515 civilians remained alive in the city.

Unbelievable acts of courage were common on both sides. One Russian survivor, Lieutenant Anton Kuzmich Dragan, described events after his unit found itself cut off from the rest of its division. Slowly, Dragan's men retreated, holing up in one building after another. "A soldier would crawl out of an occupied position," Dragan said, "only when the ground was on fire under him and his clothes were smoldering."

At last Dragan and his men took refuge in a three-story building to make their last stand. Dragan positioned his heavy machine gun with the last of its cartridges so that it could sweep the street. He was determined to use it only at the most critical moment. The first German attackers were beaten off with small arms, hand grenades, and rocks. A German officer with a megaphone appealed to the Russians to surrender. In answer, they hoisted a red flag—a vest dyed with the blood of their wounded.

Then the Russians heard a panzer approaching. Dragan sent his artilleryman out with their only antitank rifle and last three shells, but before the man could reach the tank he was captured. After about an hour, Dragan was surprised to see a unit of German infantry marching boldly up the street directly into his machine-gun sights. Somehow the captured artilleryman had convinced the Germans that the Russians were out of ammunition. Dragan corrected that impression by pumping his last 250 bullets into the Germans. Another hour passed. Then the Germans led the artilleryman to a heap of rubble in view of Dragan and his men and shot him.

In the southern part of the city equally determined acts of heroism took place. The Germans broke through several lines of defense until only the defenders of a huge grain elevator still full of grain barred their way. Under a white flag, a German officer asked the Russians to surrender the elevator, or else "in an hour's time we will bomb you out of existence."

"Tell all your Nazis to go to hell," he was told.

The expectation of taking the grain elevator in an hour proved overly optimistic, to say the least. It took a week. Shortly after the German attack began, the grain caught fire. Between the smoke and dust, the Russian defenders often could not see the Germans who entered the elevator, but they could hear them breathing and fired accordingly. At one point, a German soldier wrote, "If all the buildings in Stalingrad are defended like this, then none of our soldiers will get back to Germany."

Snipers were a plague on both sides. A man needed only to raise his head above the rubble to die. Vasily Zaitsev, a former shepherd who had perfected his marksmanship hunting deer in the Ural Mountains, registered forty kills in one ten-day period. The Germans flew in S.S. Colonel Heinz Thorwald, the head of their sniper school near Berlin, and shots from the German "master sniper" began taking their toll.

Snipers were in action all along the battlefront, but Zaitsev and Thorwald were the best each side could offer. Which would kill the other? Because experienced snipers often changed their positions, Zaitsev and Thorwald were in a strange duel, neither certain of the other's location. At last, when two veteran Russian snipers went down at the same place, Zaitsev believed he had located Thorwald. Carefully he looked over the terrain, trying to decide exactly where the German was hiding. After rejecting several possibilities, he settled on a sheet of iron beside a pile of bricks. He tested his theory by slowly raising a mitten on the end of a board. A second later came the crack of a rifle. The angle of the bullet hole in his mitten told Zaitsev he had been right—the Nazi was under the iron sheet. To lure the German into exposing himself, Zaitsev had a friend a little to the side raise his helmet. When the German fired, the friend screamed as though hit. As Zaitsev expected, the German leaned forward for a better look. The Russian fired and the Nazi master sniper was dead.

In the nightmare world of brutal, often hand-to-hand fighting, some men went crazy with fear. Others found unexpected courage. During yet another attack on the tractor factory, a German sergeant named Esser dived for cover behind a wrecked armored car. When he looked around, he saw only death. His company commander, his platoon commander, his section leader—all dead. Something inside him snapped. "Forward!" he yelled and dashed across sixty yards of open space to the factory with twelve men behind him. He blew a hole in the factory wall,

German soldiers pass by German-made generators in a destroyed Stalingrad power station. When walking through enemy territory soldiers had to be on constant alert against snipers, expert marksmen who lurked in unlikely places waiting to put a bullet through their foe.

moved inside, and mowed down the Russian defenders on the ground floor. Then he ran up the stairs and took eighty astonished Russians prisoner.

Neither side lacked courage, but slowly German superiority in equipment and manpower gained the upper hand. By late October, the Germans controlled 90 percent of the city. Sludge ice was beginning to drift down the Volga; soon the river would become impassable and the defenders would be denied even the trickle of supplies they had been receiving from Moscow. For all practical purposes the Germans had won.

But the city was not wholly in German hands. To Hitler, his victory was incomplete. He wanted Stalingrad eradicated. So he ordered the fighting to continue until every square inch of the city was under the Nazi swastika and every Russian was either dead or in chains.

At about this time, Franz Halder, the German Chief of the General Staff, wrote:

> Hitler's decisions had ceased to have anything in common with the principles of strategy and operations as they have been recognized for generations past. They were the products of a violent nature following its momentary impulses, which recognized no limits to possibility and which made its wish-dreams the father of its acts.

A few days later, Halder became yet another general fired by Hitler.

CHAPTER FOUR

Uranus

Commanding outnumbered forces, Russian general Vasily Ivanovich Chuikov made a heroic effort to hold off the September 1942 German advance on Stalingrad.

For a time in the summer of 1942 General Zhukov had been in charge of the Stalingrad defense, but before the Germans reached the city, Stalin called him back to Moscow to serve as one of the dictator's main advisers. General A. I. Yeremenko, still recovering from a leg wound suffered on the central front, was given command with Khrushchev as his political officer. One of Yeremenko's first decisions was to deal with a pontoon bridge his engineers had laboriously built on the Volga. As the only intact span across the river, the bridge could provide a much-needed supply route for Yeremenko, but should it be captured by the Germans, it would doom the entire Russian effort. Without hesitation, Yeremenko ordered it destroyed.

Once the Germans entered Stalingrad, Yeremenko and Khrushchev discovered they could not command the whole front from their bunker within the city. By telephone Khrushchev asked Stalin to allow them to move their headquarters to the northeast bank of the river. Stalin at first refused, saying that seeing the commanders leave the city would be too discouraging to the troops. Perhaps he also wanted to punish Khrushchev further for the loss at Kharkov. But eventually, Khrushchev prevailed and the overall command was moved. On September 12 the immediate command within the city was handed to an obscure general named Vasily Ivanovich Chuikov. It was Chuikov who would emerge as the greatest hero of the battle.

Chuikov was the exact opposite of Paulus, his German counterpart. Though the German's roots were middle class, "Our Most Elegant Gentleman" seemed every inch an aristocrat: carefully groomed, tall, thin, darkly handsome. One of his staff officers said he had "the face of a martyr." Chuikov, in contrast, looked like a peasant, which indeed he was: squat and broad shouldered, his thick black hair always unruly, his mouth filled with gold-capped teeth, his uniform forever in dire need of pressing. He was loud, abrasive, and crude and had no tolerance for incompetence whether below or above him in rank. But Chuikov also differed from Paulus in a more fundamental and far more important way. The German was careful to the point of being indecisive: While he considered all his options, opportunity passed. Chuikov never hesitated. When a decision was needed, he made it immediately and went on to the next. Now he promised Yeremenko, "We shall hold the city or die there."

Along a twenty-mile front, Chuikov's skeleton force faced a German army of 100,000 men. His Sixty-second Army, still reeling from the defeat that drove it into Stalingrad, was down to 50,000 men. An infantry brigade held 666 men instead of its normal 5,000. A regiment of 3,000 was actually down to only 100. One tank brigade—normally 80 tanks—had a single tank.

With a machine gun at the ready, German soldiers wait to fire on their enemy during the street fighting in Stalingrad. The combat and bombing virtually destroyed the once vital city.

The morning after Chuikov took command, the Germans launched what they expected to be their final attack. It began with a massive bombardment. Then Paulus aimed two mighty blows at the city, attacking with three infantry divisions from the west while General Hoth took two infantry divisions and two panzer divisions and slammed up from the south. The Russians staggered backward, desperate for reinforcements.

Ten thousand Russian soldiers of the elite 13th Guards were due to be ferried across the Volga to join the battle. They were crucial to the defense of the city, but the major who commanded the brigade guarding the landing area reported he had only one hundred men and a single T-34 tank. "Rally your men around the tank," Chuikov told him, "and hold the approaches to the port. If you don't hold out, I'll have you shot."

The major was killed in the subsequent fighting but the landing area was held, and the 13th Guards arrived to join the fray. Chuikov was forced to move his headquarters three times in the face of constant shelling. Before dawn on September 14, he mounted a counterattack that drove the Germans back, but with the sun came the Luftwaffe. German air superiority was enough to foil Chuikov's attack, but he had managed to keep Stalingrad from being overrun by the German assault. In the month of street fighting that followed, German progress was measured in feet and yards. But slowly Chuikov's army was forced to give ground.

By October 1942 only rubble remained where once there had been a thriving city with schools, businesses, factories, and a curious water-spouting crocodile statue in the town square. Electricity, water, and sewage were unreliable in much of the city, gone completely in some parts. The half million inhabitants either had fled across the Volga, lay dead beneath the stones, or had taken up arms alongside the Red Army. There were no mere civilians, only fighters and the dead. The Germans held 90 percent of a city rendered absolutely worthless to them, at great cost: 7,700 German dead, 31,000 wounded.

The generals on both sides were exhibiting telltale signs of stress. Paulus had developed a facial tic he no longer bothered to hide. Chuikov was afflicted with a nervous eczema on his arms and hands. Again and again Chuikov begged Moscow for more troops and more arms; only trickles of either arrived. Then large slabs of ice began floating down the Volga. Until the river froze solid and supplies could be delivered across the ice, Chuikov would receive no supplies at all. He must hold with what little he had left.

Meanwhile, the powerful German Sixth Army represented the cream of what Hitler called the master race. After the war, Chuikov described his opponent:

> The Sixth Army . . . was no ordinary army. It contained twenty-two divisions with reinforcements, more than twice the size of a normal army. Hitler boasted about its maneuverability and its power as a shock-force, its personnel—officers and men. The divisions of the army were composed of "pure Aryans." For example, the 79th Infantry Division was formed in August 1942 almost exclusively of soldiers between twenty and twenty-seven years old. The prisoners themselves told us that one in every five soldiers was a Nazi Party member.

By mid-October, Chuikov was reduced to defending a narrow, eight-mile-long, two-mile-wide strip along the river. The tractor factory was lost. Germans pushed through to the bank of the Volga, cutting the Russian defense in two. Still Chuikov fought on.

Uranus Begins

What Chuikov did not know was that the maddening sparseness of reinforcements and supplies was part of a plan hatched by Generals Zhukov and General Alexander Vasilevsky, another member of the Russian general staff, and approved by Stalin in early September. The so-called Moscow Solution, code-named

Uranus, was shrouded in deepest secrecy. Only Zhukov, Vasilevsky, and Stalin knew its full extent.

According to Uranus, Stalingrad was to be held with the most minimal force possible while the Germans wore themselves down. Hence, Chuikov was slated to receive no more men or machines than were absolutely necessary to keep his toehold in Stalingrad. The Sixty-second Army would take a horrible beating, but at the same time it would keep Paulus's army pinned in the city and exact its toll in German casualties.

Every Available Man

In the meantime, every available man, tank, gun, or plane was assembled in secret to provide a force capable of delivering a single, overwhelming, knockout blow to the Germans. Units were brought in under the cover of night from as far as Siberia. Vehicles ran without lights. When daylight came, trucks, tanks, guns, and men were stashed in ravines or forests under camouflage nets to hide them from the prying eyes of the Luftwaffe. Though the Germans were aware of a buildup, they never dreamed of its massive size. The target date for Uranus was set for mid-November.

The Russians knew that the cream of Paulus's forces were in Stalingrad. But to the north and south, Paulus's flanks were held mostly by Hungarian, Romanian, and Italian troops who did not compare to the veteran German units in training, experience, equipment, or enthusiasm. Uranus would be launched against these weak flanks.

On November 9 the Germans flew four battalions of specially trained combat engineers—twenty-four hundred men—into Stalingrad. These units were experts in the demolition of large fortifications. Paulus put them in the forefront of what he yet again expected to be his final assault. Two Russian strongholds, known to the German soldiers as the Chemist's Shop and the Red House, were the key to victory. Again and again, Russian defenders had stymied German attacks at those two points. This time the combat engineers were able to overrun the Chemist's Shop quickly, but the Red House would not yield. For four days the defenders there stopped Paulus's advance cold. When at last the Germans burst into the house and killed the last defenders, who had taken refuge in the cellar, the assault had been blunted: By then, the Russians were entrenched in their next line of defense. Once more the fighting returned to house-to-house slogging.

At 7:32 A.M. on November 19, Chuikov and the defenders heard the sound of heavy bombardment far to the northwest. Their long agony was coming to an end; Uranus had begun.

Despite the great secrecy surrounding the Russian buildup, the Germans had assumed an offensive was being readied along the lines of the previous winter's counterattack at Moscow, but they did not think it would amount to much. Still, scattered reports of a growing Russian force continued. On November 10 Hitler, who consistently underestimated the strength of his enemies, ordered the 22nd Panzer Division, which had been kept in reserve 150 miles to the south, to reinforce the Romanians along the Don. The division's 104 tanks had been dug in and buried in straw to protect them from the bitter cold. But mice had nested in the straw and gnawed the insulation on exposed electrical wires, causing short circuits. When the crews tried to start their tanks, 39 would not kick over at all, and others soon were stopped on the road. In all, only 42 of 104 panzers reached their objective.

A few days before Uranus, Paulus issued a morale-building pronouncement to his men: "It is unlikely that the Russians will fight with the same strength as last winter." He could not have been more wrong. On November 19 he faced a Russian army of more than a million men, 13,451 cannon, 900 tanks, and 1,115 airplanes.

The attack, under Major General Nikolai Vatutin, began at Serafimovich on the Don about one hundred miles northwest of Stalingrad, where the Russians had maintained a bridgehead across the river. After an eighty-minute, 3,500-gun softening barrage, the Fifth Tank and Twenty-first Armies exploded southeast into the Romanian Third Army. The weather was perfect for the Russians, a mixture of snow and fog that grounded the Luftwaffe. Dressed in white, the Russian infantrymen were nearly invisible as they advanced. Tanks steering by compass rolled irresistibly forward, suddenly appearing out of the fog spouting machine-gun fire. Some of the Romanians fought with surprising valor, but many succumbed to "tank fright" and ran for their lives. It made little difference; the poorly trained and even more poorly equipped Romanians were no match for the overwhelming force unleashed against them.

The mouse-damaged 22nd Panzer under General Ferdinand Heim gave a good account of itself. Suddenly coming upon a division of Russian tanks twice their number, the panzers, with the advantage of surprise, destroyed 26 T-34s in a brisk fight. If all 104 of the division's panzers had been on the scene, the Russian attack might have stalled. But Heim had no way to protect his flanks. In danger of being encircled, he disengaged and moved his panzers west to safety across the Chir River. It was a wise move smartly executed.

Russian soldiers don hooded parkas that keep them warm and allow them to blend into the snowy landscape.

But that was not the way Hitler saw it. To the führer, Heim had retreated. Accusing the general of rank cowardice, Hitler had Heim flown back to Berlin, stripped of his rank, court-martialed, and imprisoned.

By the end of the first day of the attack, the Russians had torn a fifty-mile-wide gap in their enemy's line.

The Second Attack

From the beginning Zhukov and Vasilevsky had planned Uranus as a two-pronged attack. The first blow under Vatutin rolled southeast from Serafimovich. The next day, November 20, the second sledgehammer strike, made up of the Fifty-first and Fifty-seventh Armies under Yeremenko, smashed northwest from below Stalingrad against a line held by the Romanian Fourth Army and the German Fourth Panzer Army. Delaying the southern attack by one day was a deliberate tactic aimed at cutting off Paulus in Stalingrad. The Russians feared that if both prongs were launched simultaneously, Paulus would recognize the danger and retreat east to escape encirclement. In view of Hitler's rigid attitude toward any kind of retreat, however, the Russians need not have worried.

Yeremenko, too, wanted to wait until the German reserves were fully committed to stopping the attack from the north. He asked for several days' grace instead of just one but was told the attack must begin on the 20th. Still, the less than enthusiastic Yeremenko did not begin his pre-attack bombardment until 10:00 in the morning. He was surprised, not to say overjoyed, when the Romanians in front of him fled in panic. Within a few hours he reported taking more than ten thousand prisoners.

The German 29th Motorized Infantry Division was a far tougher opponent. Charging toward the sound of guns, the division's fifty-five tanks came upon ninety Russian tanks and began firing at four hundred yards. The Russians were caught off guard and confused. They seldom handled surprise encounters well, and this was no exception. Within minutes, dozens of T-34s were ablaze while others raced around trying to evade the withering cannonade. Not far away, a trainload of Russian infantry heading to the front also fell under the guns of the 29th.

Just when it seemed the Russian attack might be stopped, the 29th was ordered to move east and take up defensive positions at Stalingrad. At Army Group B's headquarters, it had been determined that Yeremenko's thrust was aimed at the city. This was a terrible miscalculation. Yeremenko's goal was Kalach, where he planned to link up with Vatutin charging down from the northwest. Now he simply swung his army in a wide uppercut, bypassing the entrenched German positions. On the first day, he gained thirty miles. At this point the attack was unstoppable.

The Russian Counteroffensive

At Kalach on the Don River, the Germans had set up a gunnery school. Every morning, panzers would roll across the vital bridge to the west side of the river, where they practiced their marksmanship. The guards had grown used to this ritual. On the morning of November 22, tanks appeared and were casually waved on by the sleepy guards. Three tanks had crossed and two more were on the bridge when suddenly one of the tanks on the west shore began firing its machine guns. Too late the guards realized that the tanks they had sent across the bridge were Russian. The Germans reacted and knocked out several tanks, but the damage had been done. Russian reinforcements were rushed forward. Yeremenko was in possession of the key bridge across the Don. The way was open to link with Vatutin. On November 23 units of Vatutin's and Yeremenko's armies joined at Kalach.

The onslaught had cost the Russians one hundred thousand casualties, but they had killed an estimated ninety-five thousand Germans and taken seventy-two thousand prisoners. In the days that followed, a great deal of bloody fighting ensued as the Soviets spread out to the east and west, enlarging and reinforcing their positions. It was far from a walkover; but fortunately for the Russians as they slowly tightened their death grip on Stalingrad, they had a great deal of help from Hitler.

The Master Strategist

General Paulus was no fool, but his hands were tied by his führer. The day after the attack began, he started moving his forces west to a more defensible position along the Chir River, a tributary of the Don. Hitler immediately ordered him back to Stalingrad. Two days later, when it became obvious that the northern and southern prongs would meet and leave him encircled, he asked for permission to break out of the trap. Hitler refused. "Sixth Army must know that I am doing everything to help and to relieve it. I shall issue my orders in good time."

One of Paulus's officers decided to take matters into his own hands. General Walter von Seydlitz-Kurzbach, commander of the 94th Infantry Division, reasoned that a retreat once begun would turn into a stampede. Orders or not, the Sixth Army would extricate itself from the trap. All it needed was a start. And that, he would supply. In preparation, he set his fuel and ammunition dumps ablaze, blew up his bunkers, and burned all secret papers. But the fires attracted the Russians, who fell upon the 94th before it could even begin its retreat. Hundreds of Seydlitz-Kurzbach's men were slaughtered.

By November 22, Paulus's Sixth Army—250,000 men—was surrounded. Yet all was not yet lost. The thin line of Russians between the Sixth Army and safety to the west could still be breached. Paulus was perhaps the German general least likely to disagree with Adolf Hitler, but he nevertheless sent his stark assessment of the situation to the führer. Unless he was allowed to break out immediately, disaster loomed. Came the inevitable reply: The Sixth Army would hold its position on the Volga. Incredibly, Paulus was told his army would henceforth be supplied by air.

If ever there was a time when one of Hitler's underlings told him what he wanted to hear in defiance of facts, this was it. Blustering Hermann Göring, the head of the Luftwaffe, airily promised Hitler that his planes could fully supply the Sixth Army. When told that would require a minimum of five hundred tons of supplies a day even if the Sixth's horses were slaughtered for food, Göring continued to insist that it could be done. When General von Richthofen heard about Göring's boast, he called it "stark, raving madness!"

Nazi troops and their horses trudge through snow and ankle-deep mud. Lacking warm coats and boots, the Germans found themselves unprepared for the harsh Russian winter.

Hitler and Napoléon

In the wake of Stalingrad, inevitable comparisons were drawn between Hitler's defeat in Russia and Napoléon's equally unsuccessful invasion of that country in 1812. Like Hitler, the French emperor commanded most of Europe, but also like Hitler, he had not been able to conquer England and turned instead to the east. The parallels continued in that at first Napoléon advanced across the Russian plain almost at will. And, just as they would do 130 years later, the Russians put everything in his path to the torch.

But, unlike Hitler, Napoléon not only reached the gates of Moscow, he actually captured the city. However, he discovered his victory was worthless. Nearly everything of value had been removed to safety by the "defeated" Russians and what was left was burned to the ground.

With the awful Russian winter coming on, Napoléon turned his army toward home. It was on the retreat that he actually was defeated. Russian snipers picked off French troops along the way. Mounted cossacks swept in with surprise attacks on the long, undefendable French column. Artillery continually shelled the retreating soldiers. Supplies were exhausted, and the scorched land yielded little to foragers. And then winter, the Russians' greatest ally, arrived. French troops starved and froze and were continually harassed by snipers. Of the 650,000 troops Napoléon took into Russia, only about 40,000 returned to France. It was a defeat from which he could not recover. Within two years, his empire was destroyed and he was sent into exile.

Hitler's worst blunder was his refusal to allow strategic retreats; Napoléon's retreat turned into a catastrophe. But unlike Hitler, Napoléon was a courageous and brilliant soldier who shared the hardships with his men. During the worst moments, he was there to urge his soldiers on. Without his inspiring presence and generalship, perhaps none of his men would have survived.

Nevertheless, like Hitler, Napoléon's Russian campaign led to his destruction.

In the first place, Göring did not have enough airplanes. Planners estimated that it would take 1,000 trimotor Junker 52s, the standard German transport, flying every day with full loads to feed and arm Paulus's men and fuel their vehicles. Yet in all the Luftwaffe, from Africa to Norway, there were only 750 Ju-52s. Furthermore, the awful Russian winter kept those that were on the scene grounded for days. When they were in the air, they had to fly over Russian-held territory to reach Stalingrad, and the slow-moving transports were choice targets for Russian antiaircraft guns and pursuit planes. November 29 was a particularly good case in point: 59 airplanes were sent to Stalingrad that day; only 25 arrived. At Stalingrad the Germans held two airstrips but both were small and in bad repair, causing numerous crack-ups. And because the proud Luftwaffe refused to let the army quartermaster corps oversee its operations, ridiculous mistakes were made. One day planes delivered eight thousand right shoes but no left ones. Instead of the promised five hundred tons of supplies a day, Göring's airmen seldom delivered more than one hundred tons. By mid-December they were averaging fewer than eighty-five tons a day.

Everything the Sixth Army needed was in short supply. Hitler had expected a quick, warm-weather victory and as a consequence his army lacked winter coats, uniforms, boots, socks, stoves, and other basic protections from the awful cold. The Russians faced the same freezing temperatures, of course, but they were better equipped to handle it. Illness, increased by the appalling conditions, was rampant, but the German doctors had little medicine.

Even ammunition had to be hoarded. One day a German sergeant in charge of an antitank gun saw three T-34s approaching. Three well-aimed rounds stopped them. Then more tanks appeared. The sergeant beat them off with fifteen shots. But instead of commending him, his commander upbraided him for expending too much ammunition.

The worst shortage was food. First the Germans ate the horses. Soon Paulus's men were catching mice and even rats. On December 9 the first two German soldiers starved to death.

A Relief Attempt

Field Marshal Erich von Manstein was perhaps the most able general on the Russian front. One of the architects of the blitzkrieg in France and the conqueror of Sevastopol, he was even admired by Hitler, it was said, at least to the extent that Hitler admired anyone other than himself. When Uranus began, Manstein was at Leningrad trying to bring that seemingly endless siege to a conclusion. At the end of November, he was ordered south to take command of the newly created Army Group Don and organize the relief of the Sixth Army. The Sixth's morale took an upswing. "Manstein is coming! Manstein is coming!" troops called to each other.

The plan called for Manstein to fight his way to Stalingrad, opening up a narrow corridor down which supplies and arms would be rushed to Paulus. Once it was rearmed, the Sixth would break out of its trap through the same corridor. By now even Hitler could no doubt see that the only way to save the Sixth Army was to let it abandon Stalingrad. Yet, although this was clearly a necessary part of the plan, he refused to issue an actual breakout order.

Manstein efficiently began gathering his trucks and supplies, but he found that Army Group Don consisted mostly of remnants and leftovers from various armies. The single largest fighting force under his command was the surrounded Sixth Army! He demanded more and better units.

Meanwhile, the 11th Panzer Division under General Hermann Balck was rushed up from the south. Balck was a feisty and capable fighter and the 11th was a crack unit. Almost immediately it found itself embroiled in a bloody battle with a Soviet tank column. When darkness came, the Russians dug in for the night. Not so Balck. He whipped his tanks out of the line, leaving only a few cannons to fire occasionally to make the Russians believe they still had tanks in front of them. Then Balck's tanks made a wide circle and came up behind the Russians at dawn. Before them was a long Soviet supply column, chugging peacefully toward the front. Using only their machine guns, Balck's tanks swept in beside the column and destroyed it utterly. They moved on to attack the Russian tanks from the rear. The surprised Russians lost fifty-three T-34s while Balck sustained only light losses.

Manstein's relief force fought its way toward Stalingrad. By December 20 it was only thirty-five miles from the city, but that was as far as it would go. The sheer weight of Russian opposition, the bitter cold, and dwindling fuel supplies brought the effort to a halt. To Manstein, the only chance to save even a fraction of the Sixth Army was for Paulus to drive outward and link with the relief force. He urged Paulus to attempt a breakout, but Paulus pleaded that his army was too weakened to succeed; he would attempt the move only if Hitler ordered it. Manstein tried in vain to

German Sixth Army Trapped at Stalingrad

Kremenskaya

Kletskaya

The Russians surround Paulus's Sixth Army, Nov. 22, 1942.

Chernyshevskaya

Rynok

STALINGRAD

Kalach

Leninsk

Raigorod

Nizhne Chirskaya

Plodovitoye

Tovmosin

Abganerova

Zhutovo

Manstein's relief plan.

GERMAN FRONT UNTIL NOVEMBER 20, 1942.

RUSSIAN COUNTER-OFFENSIVE

GERMAN ARMY

SCALE OF MILES

0   50

convince Hitler to order the breakout. He flew his intelligence chief into Stalingrad to reason with Paulus. The officer was told that the Sixth Army would still be there by Easter; all it lacked was supplies. Between the führer sitting in Berlin and the general sitting in Stalingrad, the Sixth Army was condemned to death.

An Army Dies

The possibility of saving Paulus and the Sixth Army ended when the Russians launched another attack aimed at trapping the German forces in the Caucasus. Manstein was forced to break off his relief effort to counter this new Russian offensive, one that threatened to end the war in a single move.

In Stalingrad, German soldiers continued to die. Rations for each German were down to two ounces of bread and a soup made mostly of water for lunch. For dinner, the lucky man might have a slice or two of canned meat. More likely, he would have only more watery soup.

On Christmas Eve, the Sixth Army's soldiers made meager attempts at celebration. One man had carved a beautiful wooden Christmas tree. Others produced less artistic trees from pieces of metal decorated with scraps of paper or cloth. Carols were sung and red, green, and white flares were fired into the sky. Many men spent the evening writing letters home—letters that said in one way or another they knew the end was near. "Nothing can happen to me any longer," wrote one man. "I have made my peace with God."

On Christmas Day 1942, a blizzard propelled by fifty-mile-an-hour winds tore through the city, followed by a heavy barrage of mortars, cannons, and Soviet Katyusha rockets and several T-34 attacks. When the sun set, 1,280 German soldiers had died on Christendom's holiest day.

Daily, Russian airplanes dropped leaflets on the Sixth Army bearing the telling message, "Every seven seconds a German dies in Russia." Loudspeakers were put in place to blare the same grim statistic toward the German lines. The Russians sent a subtler but even more effective message to the Germans by setting up field kitchens in places where they knew prevailing winds would waft the delicious smells of cooking food across to their starving enemy.

Still, the Germans fought hard against the Russian attacks. In the midst of fighting, a soldier might almost forget his hunger or the unbelievable cold. But in the quiet moments between battles the twin killers could not be ignored. Slowly the realization dawned on even the most faithful Nazis: Their führer had abandoned them to their fate.

The German airlift, steadily dwindling for weeks, ended altogether when the Russians captured the last airstrip. Toward the end, the chief job of the few airplanes that reached Stalingrad was to take out wounded. The worst cases were to go out first, but on more than one occasion men with less severe wounds stormed the planes attempting to escape.

The men of the Sixth Army reacted to the hopeless situation in different ways. Most went about their business in a near zombie state, but suicide became common. A few officers ordered a trusted subordinate to kill them. Many men chose the more indirect method of one young officer, who grabbed a machine gun and stood exposed on a heap of rubble firing at the Russian lines until he was cut down by return fire.

On January 22, 1943, Paulus sent a plaintive message to Hitler: "The Russians are advancing on a six-kilometer frontage. There is no possibility of closing the gap. All provisions are used up. Over 12,000 unattended wounded men in the pocket. What orders am I to issue the troops who have no ammunition left?"

As always, Hitler blustered. "The troops will defend their positions to the last. The Sixth Army has thus made a historic contribution in the most gigantic war effort in German history."

Hitler played one last cynical card. As the end of January 1943 approached, he promoted Paulus to the rank of field marshal. No German field marshal had ever surrendered in battle. Paulus was being told to die fighting, a brave end whose propaganda value was not lost on the Nazis.

But Paulus refused to cooperate.

On January 31 a young Russian artillery lieutenant named Fyodor Yelchenko was bombarding the rubble that had once been Stalingrad's Univermag department store when a German officer popped his head out of a door. "Our big chief wants to talk to your big chief," the German yelled. Yelchenko called back that the Russian big chief was busy fighting just then. If the Germans wanted to talk, it would be to Yelchenko.

Accompanied by two of his men, Yelchenko was taken to the basement of the department store, where he found hundreds of dirty, starving Germans. Unknown to him, he had been bombarding Paulus's headquarters. He was taken to a small room in the back of the basement where he found the always immaculate field marshal lying on a cot in a rumpled uniform, unshaven. Paulus asked for surrender terms.

"That finishes it," Yelchenko said.

CHAPTER FIVE

On to Berlin

In the seven-month period from mid-1942 through January 1943, the outcome of World War II was sealed. What had for so long looked like an Axis triumph was changed to an inevitable victory for the Allies.

Following Pearl Harbor—December 7, 1941—the Japanese spent six months advancing pell-mell across the Pacific, capturing Indonesia, the Philippines, and numerous small islands. Australia came under air attack and was threatened with invasion. But in early June 1942 in a three-day sea battle the U.S. Navy defeated a huge enemy aircraft carrier force near Midway, a tiny island northwest of Hawaii, sinking four Japanese aircraft carriers while losing only one. Midway stopped the Japanese advance and severely crippled its navy. In August, U.S. Marines landed on the island of Guadalcanal and began the slow and bloody task of retaking the Pacific one island at a time.

By mid-1942 German general Erwin Rommel had advanced across North Africa to the point where he threatened the Suez Canal, Great Britain's lifeline to the East. The Desert Fox, as Rommel was known, was a brilliant tank commander, and his Afrika Corps won victory after victory. But in October, British tank forces under Field Marshal Bernard Montgomery defeated Rommel at El Alamein in western Egypt. Rommel was driven west in retreat

As the end of World War II drew nearer, British troops defeated Erwin Rommel at El Alamein in Egypt.

British prime minister Winston Churchill argued against Stalin's request for an Allied invasion of France in 1942. Churchill feared that such a move would be detrimental to his British troops and recommended waiting until the German armies were more vulnerable.

only to find Allied troops landing behind him in Algeria and Morocco on November 8. Germany's African adventure ended in defeat. Hitler recalled Rommel to Germany but left most of the vaunted Afrika Corps to its fate.

Midway and El Alamein were important victories for the Allies, but the crucial test was Stalingrad.

From the beginning Allied leaders had determined that despite Japan's victories in the Pacific, Germany was the more dangerous enemy and must be defeated first. The United States and the United Kingdom would fight in the Pacific—Russia had not declared war on the Japanese—but their major effort was to be directed against Hitler. And ultimately he must be defeated on the continent of Europe.

As soon as Russia was in the war, Stalin began lobbying for a "second front," that is, an invasion of Europe by Great Britain and the United States. Only then, he insisted, would Hitler be forced to draw sufficient armies from the eastern front to enable the Russians to beat Germany. The Allies sent him thousands of tons of supplies, but they were not strong enough through 1942 to attack across the English Channel themselves. President Roosevelt and his military advisers favored an invasion of France as soon as possible, but British prime minister Winston Churchill believed an invasion from England would be suicidal until the German armies of "Fortress Europe" were more vulnerable. Stalin, who trusted no one, looked with great suspicion at the Allied leaders, particularly Churchill, a longtime foe of communism. He believed Churchill was holding off a European invasion until Russia was bled white so that when victory was finally achieved the Soviet Union would be irredeemably weakened.

It was a tragic catch-22: Stalin maintained a second front was needed for a Russian victory but Churchill insisted no second front was possible without a Russian victory. To that end, he was willing to send tons of British- and American-made equipment across the North Sea to Russia, even though Great Britain needed to build its own forces. Then, in the summer of 1942, a large convoy taking supplies to Russia lost more than two-thirds of its ships to German planes and submarines. Churchill cancelled all convoys to Russia until the weather turned bad enough to give the ships some protection from German planes. To Stalin, who tended to ignore all Allied losses except his own, it was a stab in the back. His anger threatened to upset the fragile Allied alliance.

On August 12, 1942, just as the Battle of Stalingrad was beginning to take shape, Churchill flew to Moscow. In a brutally frank, seven-hour conversation between the two old enemies, Stalin and Churchill achieved not friendship but enough mutual respect to continue their alliance. The convoys began again and the supplies they delivered made a difference in the outcome at Stalingrad.

The Cost

After Paulus surrendered, thousands of unburied bodies lay frozen in Stalingrad and out on the Russian steppe. Nikita Khrushchev put together a unit of Russian soldiers and German prisoners to gather the bodies. There were too many for burial. Instead they were stacked between layers of railroad ties and burned. Later Khrushchev wrote, "I went once to watch, but I didn't go a second time. Napoléon or someone once said that burning enemy corpses smell good. Well, speaking for myself I don't agree. It was a very unpleasant smell and altogether a very unpleasant scene."

Although statistics vary, the cost to both sides at Stalingrad was appalling. One estimate placed Soviet casualties for the entire Stalingrad campaign at 750,000 killed and wounded. The Germans lost fewer men but they were far more difficult to replace. The Sixth Army began with 250,000 men. As many as 35,000 were flown to safety, most of them severely wounded. At

After the Red Army's victory over the Germans, the devastation of Hitler's armies remained as silent testimony to the fierce fighting that occurred at Stalingrad.

least 125,000 died within the confines of Stalingrad itself. When Paulus surrendered, 90,000 German troops became Russian prisoners. They were not treated well. Only about 6,000 ever returned to Germany. Marshal Zhukov claimed German losses in the whole area totaled a million and a half men, 3,500 tanks, 12,000 guns, and 3,000 aircraft. Zhukov's figures are no doubt greatly inflated, yet even halved they represent the greatest defeat the Wehrmacht had ever suffered.

The psychological losses to the Wehrmacht were almost as terrible as the losses in men and machines. A great army of pure Aryans had been destroyed by what the Nazis insisted was an inferior race. In the Nazis' mad theories of a master race such a result was inconceivable. Yet, if it could happen once . . . Stalingrad dealt a blow to Wehrmacht confidence, one from which it never completely recovered.

Germany's greatest victories had been achieved by the Wehrmacht's ability to move rapidly and strike quickly—the blitzkrieg. It was an army trained to attack. After Stalingrad, Germany essentially fought defensively for the remainder of the war. Although Hitler continued to talk of victory, most of his military leaders understood that the war could no longer be won. All that could be hoped for was to make the Allies pay such a high price for victory that they would settle for a generous peace.

And what can be said of the master strategist Adolf Hitler? Was not his fixation on destroying Stalingrad based on a personal whim rather than sound military judgment? Was not his intransigent order that there was to be no strategic retreat ultimately responsible for trapping the Sixth Army? What of his incredible decision to supply the Sixth Army by air when every responsible German officer knew such a feat was impossible? And in the end, had he not simply abandoned the Sixth Army to its fate? Until Stalingrad, even those German officers who considered Hitler an upstart had been forced to admit his military instincts had been unerring. But with the defeat came doubt. A year later, a ring of officers attempted unsuccessfully to assassinate their führer.

Stalingrad effected great changes within the Soviet Union, too. Some were cosmetic. Officers' uniforms, plain and drab since the tsar had been removed, suddenly sprouted epaulets, sashes, ribbons, and yards of gold braid. The new adornments were signs of the Russian army's newfound pride and confidence.

"At the beginning of the war," explained one Russian tank com-

In an unsuccessful attempt to assassinate Hitler, German officers bombed the führer's headquarters. Here, Hermann Göring surveys the site of the explosion that killed several officers but left Hitler unharmed.

The Plot to Kill Hitler

As the war began to go badly for Germany, some army officers came to believe that the only hope of salvation for their country was to rid Germany of Hitler. The Allies had sworn to prosecute the war until Germany's unconditional surrender. The officers knew that Hitler, who still ranted about victory, would never agree to that. If he continued as Germany's leader, their country would be completely destroyed. Therefore, they determined to assassinate him, set up a new government, reveal the truth of the Third Reich to a German public raised on propaganda, and surrender to the Allies.

The plot had little chance of success even had the assassination itself succeeded. The plotters were too few, and those loyal to Hitler, including the mass of German people, were too many. Nevertheless, on July 20, 1944, the leader of the plot, Lieutenant Colonel Klaus von Stauffenberg, attended a staff meeting called by the führer. In his briefcase was a time bomb.

Five minutes before the bomb was set to go off, Stauffenberg placed his briefcase within six feet of Hitler and excused himself from the meeting to make an urgent telephone call. No sooner had he left than another officer who was trying to read a map on the planning table moved the briefcase out of his way to the far side of one of the table's heavy supporting legs. That chance act saved Hitler's life. The bomb exploded, killing and injuring many officers around the table, but Hitler was barely touched.

In the aftermath of the botched attempt, Hitler had the plotters hunted down, tortured, and killed. Stauffenberg was sent before a firing squad. Others were strangled with piano wire. Reportedly Hitler had some of the most gruesome executions filmed and watched them at his leisure. Field Marshal Erwin Rommel, Germany's most famous and most successful officer, was forced to commit suicide as a coconspirator. Hitler kept any word of the popular Rommel's involvement secret and gave him an elaborate state funeral. Some suspected plotters were paraded through show trials. In all, nearly five thousand officers and party officials were executed, several thousand more than could possibly have been involved.

---

mander, "everything was done in a hurry and time was always lacking. Now we go calmly into action."

Much of the average soldier's confidence came from knowing that his commanders were competent. Generals who owed their positions to their Communist Party loyalty were out. The men who had been tested and proven at Stalingrad—Chuikov and Yeremenko—were in. Zhukov and Vasilevsky were raised to the rank of field marshal. The others were promoted within a year.

Victory brought a change in Stalin's public image, as well. Through the first years of fighting, he kept a low profile, seldom appearing in public and rarely addressing the people on the radio. Communiques were likely to be issued under Zhukov's name or that of another general or party leader. But after the victory at Stalingrad, he was suddenly everywhere—radio, wall posters, being quoted in *Pravda*. Always he was photographed in his military uniform, emphasizing his responsibility for the victory. It was made crystal clear to the Russian people that it was his courage, his daring, his strategy that had produced the triumph. Eventually he would give himself the exalted rank of *generalissimo*. Never before and never again would Joseph Stalin be as popular as he was in the days after Stalingrad.

In America patriotic political cartoonists depicted the Russian dictator as "Uncle Joe," the sort of warmhearted relative everyone in the family loves and invites to dinner. Such cartoons may have helped the war effort by promoting friendly feelings toward an ally, but the cold-blooded Stalin was as much kindly Uncle Joe as the big, bad wolf was Grandma.

Operation Star

Even before the fight for Stalingrad ended, Zhukov produced a plan that promised to deal the Germans an even greater blow. Christened Operation Star, its aim was to cut off and destroy the German forces in the Caucasus as well as Manstein's Army Group Don. It was this attack that caused Manstein to break off his attempt to rescue the Sixth Army, for he realized that should Star succeed, the results would be even more catastrophic than the loss at Stalingrad. If his force and those in the Caucasus were destroyed, the road to Berlin would lie virtually undefended.

To foil the Russian advance, Manstein needed to be able to maneuver, but as always Hitler refused to authorize even one step of withdrawal. Manstein confronted Hitler at the führer's headquarters in Rastenburg in East Prussia. He had come well prepared and presented his case for a quick withdrawal and repositioning of his army. Then he patiently countered each of Hitler's arguments against a strategic retreat. At last Hitler was left with only his belief that the spring thaw would surely stop the Russians. Manstein quietly observed that he would not bet the fate of his army on the vagaries of Russian weather. At last, Hitler gave in. Manstein flew back to his command free to maneuver.

But at first that seemed small consolation. The Russians had a huge advantage in numbers. Manstein radioed Hitler that he was outnumbered eight to one. Hitler replied that he would send thirty-seven trainloads of men and supplies. His promise had no basis in reality. Only six trainloads arrived.

In two prongs the Russians pushed west and southwest as the Germans in the Caucasus scrambled to escape the trap. Russian confidence grew as Kharkov was recaptured after a bloody fight. It appeared that the Germans were in full-scale retreat. A concerned and angry Hitler flew to Manstein's headquarters at Zaporozhye. Only a few days before he had given Manstein control of the entire southern command. Now he was ready to fire him. He quickly discovered the situation was worse than he had feared. The Russians were advancing in all directions. For once the führer made a decision about a general with his head instead of his emotions. This was surely not the time to fire Manstein, perhaps the one German general on the scene with the skill and audacity to reverse the situation. Instead, Hitler contented himself with firing the poor officer who had been entrusted with the impossible task of defending Kharkov. Manstein had a plan for a counterattack, but Hitler wanted Kharkov recaptured instead. While the general and the führer went back and forth, the Russians continued to advance. When at last Hitler gave his consent to Manstein's plan and flew back to Germany, Russian tanks were only six miles away.

Manstein's plan was risky. He concentrated all his mobile forces into five panzer commands. That gave him a powerful attack force to smash the advancing Russians, but it also meant weakening much of his defensive line. Timing was crucial. He had to send the Red Army reeling before it could take advantage of the soft spots in his line. The day after Hitler left his headquarters, Manstein launched his attack with the terse order, "The Soviet Sixth Army is to be defeated."

He had two things going for him. First, the Russians had outrun their supply lines, leaving their tanks starved for fuel and low on ammunition. Second, the Russian high command believed the Germans were in full retreat and incapable of a counterattack in force. Both the Russians' overconfidence and lack of fuel seriously restricted their ability to react. General M. M. Popov realized almost immediately he was facing more than a rear guard action when his armor came under attack by the XL Panzer Corps. He asked headquarters for permission to withdraw. This time it was the Russians who were foolishly unbending. Vatutin radioed back accusing Popov of a lack of energy and ordering him to attack. Three German divisions began cutting Popov's force into mincemeat, but he received further instructions to "annihilate" the enemy.

Manstein had achieved surprise but at great risk. At one point Russian tanks were within a few miles of his headquarters. His luck held. The tanks ran out of fuel and German gunners destroyed them where they sat.

Outnumbered and Outgunned

Across the front, the Germans were outnumbered and outgunned, but by concentrating his forces at key points Manstein was able to achieve a strategic advantage. Favorable reports poured in: 9,000 Russians captured, 23,000 killed. By one estimate, during the battle the Russians lost 615 tanks, 400 artillery pieces, 600 antitank guns, and suffered more than 100,000 killed and wounded. The Soviet offensive was stopped dead in its tracks and turned back. The threatened German armies in the Caucasus were able to retreat safely northwest.

Now Manstein turned north toward Kharkov to realize Hitler's fervent wish that the city be recaptured. After three days of vicious street fighting, Kharkov fell to Manstein on March 15. He then drove fifty miles farther north and captured the smaller city of Belograd.

Ironically, the sides had reversed themselves wishing for the spring thaw. Only a few weeks earlier, the possibility of movement-stopping mud had seemed the only thing capable of saving the German army from obliteration. Now it was the Russians who prayed for the thaw.

Their prayers were answered in the third week of March 1943. The thaw turned the Russian roads and fields into gooey, impassable swamps of mud. Trucks sank to their hubcaps in slop; tanks sat immobile while their tracks turned uselessly. Simply walking one hundred yards through the stuff took an enormous effort. A soldier could arrive at his destination with muck caked up to his thighs. When he scraped it away, he might discover that one of his boots was missing, sucked off in a mudhole. The men said that General Mud had taken over. The battle was ended for a while. It was time to take stock.

Nazi soldiers attempt to pull one of their horses out of the thick mud. An early spring thaw in 1943 turned the Russian roads and fields into boot-sucking muck, delaying the German attack.

Profit and Loss

After all the fighting, all the suffering, all the misery, all the death and destruction of the past year, the two armies found themselves occupying essentially the same positions they had held in early 1942. The Germans were again encamped along the Donets River. Stalingrad and the Caucasus were back in Soviet hands. In Germany, Hitler was blithely planning another offensive. Had it all been for naught?

Not really. Manstein's brilliant victory had saved the German army only temporarily. In effect, he had made it possible for the war to continue. But continuing was not winning. He knew, even if Hitler did not, that ultimate victory on the eastern front was impossible. The best he could hope for was a draw. Germany had lost too many tanks, too many guns, and far too many of its best fighting men to have any hopes of capturing Moscow or Stalingrad or the precious oil fields to the south. The Allied invasions of Italy and later France, coupled with the constant Allied pounding of German factories from the air, ensured continuing reductions in German manpower, fuel, and supplies.

And whereas the Wehrmacht had gone into the campaign of 1942 with confidence based on its string of victories, it now knew it could be beaten. Stalingrad had proved that.

Russian losses had been greater than Germany's, but the reinforced Soviet army now was buttressed by battle-hardened troops who knew how to win. Moreover, their equipment, particularly the T-34 tank, was the equal of their enemy's in effectiveness and superior in number. Russian factories were churning out tanks and guns in ever-increasing quantities while tons of food, armaments, and fuel arrived daily from the Allies across the sea. The Caucasus oil fields had been saved, guaranteeing a reliable fuel source.

It was only a matter of time before the Red Army became too powerful for the Wehrmacht to withstand. Stalingrad had turned the tide.

To the Victors

By the spring of 1943, victory in the war against Germany was all but certain. Yet, the events had to be played out. Many thousands of brave men died on both sides in the time that remained.

For the third consecutive year, Hitler demanded a summer offensive on the eastern front. In 1941 his target had been all of the Soviet Union; in 1942, he scaled down his objectives to the Ukraine and Caucasus. His 1943 campaign had a far more modest aim: the Kursk salient. About a hundred miles north of Kharkov, the Russians held the manufacturing city of Kursk. On a war map, Kursk and the area around it protruded into German-held territory like an angry thumb. It looked ripe to be hacked off. Hitler rhapsodized Kursk would be "a victory to shine out like a beacon to the world."

Some of his officers had their doubts and hoped there would be no 1943 offensive. Guderian asked him, "How many people do you think even know where Kursk is? It's a matter of profound indifference to the world whether we hold Kursk or not."

Hitler would not be dissuaded. But if he could see that Kursk was an inviting target, the Russians were also well aware of that fact. If there was any doubt, their spies told them exactly where and when the Germans would attack. For the first time since the war began, the Red Army had more men and machines than their foe. Now any element of surprise was lost to the Wehrmacht. Marshals Zhukov and Vasilevsky laid a death trap.

The Russians set up a box defense; if the Germans broke through one line of defense, they would find themselves subjected to fire from both front and rear positions. With each advance, more guns could be brought to bear. Very quickly a single German tank could find itself under fire from five different heavy guns, all of which had been carefully sighted in on every part of the battlefield.

In the days before the attack, Stalin nervously suggested several small advances might be advantageous. Zhukov and Vasilevsky stood firm, insisting that everything be held back until the Germans made their move. This they did on the afternoon of July 4 with a massive attack of three thousand panzers.

German Losses Mount

The first thing German tank crews discovered was that they had rolled into an area sown thick with mines, as many as five thousand per square mile. The mines could not destroy the German panzers, but they could knock off their treads and leave them sitting targets. Then the Russian heavy guns took over and wiped out the tanks one after another. Over the next four days, the Russians reported nearly eighteen hundred German tanks destroyed, no doubt an exaggeration but a definite indication of immense German losses.

Nevertheless, with skill and courage the Germans made slow advances. It was not until July 12 that the battle reached its climax. Six hundred German tanks, all that was left of the original force, charged into a Russian force of 850 tanks and self-propelled guns. Tanks and guns whirled in a wild melee, firing at point-blank range. Dive-bombers from both sides careened through the smoke, hurling destruction from above. Veterans who lived through that hell later admitted they had never seen anything like it. As night fell, 300 German tanks were able to limp away. The next day, Hitler called off the attack. He had no choice.

The Americans and British took little note of the Soviet victory at Kursk; their interest was caught up in the July 10 invasion

The Big Three

Reeling under Hitler's initial invasion, the USSR desperately sought to accommodate its newfound allies, Great Britain and the United States. One of its major concessions was to agree to a postwar United Nations that, it was hoped, would keep the world at peace.

However, once the tide was turned at Stalingrad, the USSR became a far more steely negotiator. While the United States and Great Britain worked toward a successful completion of the war in both Europe and the Pacific and hoped to institute a lasting peace, the USSR had a further agenda. Stalin planned to expand his borders. In addition to numerous diplomatic exchanges, wartime "Big Three" meetings were held at Tehran in Iran and Yalta in the Crimea, with Winston Churchill, the British prime minister, and Franklin D. Roosevelt, the American president, face to face with Stalin.

Churchill and Roosevelt were hardly negotiating from strength. They feared the possibility that the USSR might conclude a separate peace with Germany as the Bolsheviks had done in World War I. Instead, they wanted Russia not only to continue fighting the Nazis but also to declare war on Japan. At the time, Allied estimates were that the war in the Pacific might continue for several years after Germany was defeated. In addition, Roosevelt wanted continued Soviet cooperation in establishing the United Nations.

For his part, Stalin harped on the lack of a second front and the invasion of France, and insisted that Russia was bearing the brunt of the war. In the number of casualties, he was right.

In the course of the two meetings, Stalin agreed to continue the war to completion, declare war on Japan within three months of Germany's surrender, and support the UN movement. In effect, he gave up nothing that was not already in his plans. For his "concessions," Stalin was allowed to keep the Polish territory Russia had gained in 1940, given a free hand in the Baltic states, and promised the temporary occupation of eastern Germany.

A third Big Three meeting was held at Potsdam, outside Berlin, during the summer of 1945. By then Germany had been defeated, but Japan continued to fight. Clement Attlee had succeeded Churchill as prime minister in British elections, and Harry Truman had become U.S. president after the death of Roosevelt. Only Stalin returned. At Potsdam, the USSR was given a say in the postwar governments of the countries it had conquered during its advance on Berlin. Not surprisingly, such nations as Hungary, Romania, Bulgaria, and Czechoslovakia were soon turned into communist satellites of the USSR.

In the postwar cold war, British and American leaders were widely criticized for agreeing to Soviet domination of the lands behind what came to be known as the Iron Curtain. On the other hand, no land was handed over that the Russians did not already possess. And certainly neither American nor British citizens would have allowed their leaders to go directly from a war with Germany into a war with Russia to free those lands by force.

of Sicily. But Kursk was not only one of the largest armored battles ever; it was one of the most important of the war. It was the exclamation point added to Stalingrad. The tide had not only turned; it could never be reversed.

It is fair to say that the Russian victory at Stalingrad followed by the second victory at Kursk made it possible for the Allies to open a second front. Hitler was forced to rush reinforcements east and thus weaken Fortress Europe in the west. While the battle for Kursk raged, Allied forces landed on the island of Sicily at the toe of the Italian boot. In September they invaded Italy itself. Mussolini was thrown out of office—eventually he was murdered by partisans—and Italy surrendered. However, German troops continued to fight the Allies as they slowly advanced up the Italian peninsula. On June 6, 1944, the long-awaited, cross-Channel invasion of France began at Normandy. Hitler's Germany was caught in a vise, the Americans and British attacking in the west, the Russians advancing in the east. By then all but Hitler and a few of his toadies knew the war was lost.

American soldiers land on the coast of France under heavy Nazi machine-gun fire.

The Soviets began systematically crunching their way into Bulgaria, Romania, Hungary, and Poland. Early in 1944 the German siege of Leningrad begun in 1941 was broken. Warsaw was captured in January 1945. Hungary surrendered in February. By April, Russian troops were in Berlin.

Almost until the end, Adolf Hitler talked of victory. The Allies would fall out among themselves and begin fighting each other, he said. New superweapons—many existing only in his imagination—would bring the Allies to their knees. He ordered armies that no longer existed into battle. His orders were always the same: Germans were to fight to the death. When, at long last, even he knew that the Reich that was to last a thousand years was destroyed, he blamed the German people. They did not "deserve" him.

On May 8, 1945, Germany surrendered. Eight days earlier, it is believed, Hitler committed suicide in his bunker beneath the rubble that was Berlin.

Of all the participants in World War II, the Soviet Union suffered the most losses. About 7,500,000 Russian military personnel died, more than twice the number of German losses. By contrast, 405,399 Americans died in battle. The number of Russian civilian deaths attributable in one way or another to the war was far higher than those on the battlefield—an estimated 19 million.

Despite such horrendous slaughter, the Soviet Union emerged from the war much stronger than it had entered it. Possessing a huge standing army, an enormous weapons industry, and a collection of obedient, if not always enthusiastic, satellite countries in those lands it had conquered on the way to Berlin, the USSR had become with the United States one of the world's two "superpowers." The various political strategies and maneuverings of these two giants dominated the world stage for the next forty-five years. If World War II can be said to have begun with World War I, it did not truly end until the close of the cold war.

For Further Reading

Nicholas Bethell and the Editors of Time-Life Books, *Russia Besieged*. Alexandria, VA: Time-Life Books, 1977. Like all the books in this series, this account of the first year of Germany's invasion of the USSR combines a reliable and readable text with exciting photos.

Vasily Ivanovich Chuikov, *The Battle for Stalingrad*. New York: Ballantine, 1964. Stalingrad's greatest hero tells his own story, not always modestly.

Editors of Time-Life Books, *The Road to Stalingrad*. Alexandria, VA: Time-Life Books, 1991. An excellent account of the German path to defeat along with the series' usual fine photographs.

Robert T. Elson and the Editors of Time-Life Books, *Prelude to War*. Alexandria, VA: Time-Life Books, 1976. The first book in this fine series follows the rise of the Nazis and Fascists as well as Japan's movement toward war.

Red Reeder, *The Story of the Second World War: The Allies Conquer (1942–45)*. New York: Hawthorn Books, 1970. A highly readable account of the major events of World War II in two volumes. The first book includes the events leading up to the war and its first dark days. The second volume tells of the triumph of the Allies.

Harrison E. Salisbury, *The Unknown War*. New York: Doubleday, 1978. Similar to the Time-Life series in that it combines a fine text and photos, the author's point is that the war in Russia is little known or understood in the United States or Great Britain.

John Shaw and the Editors of Time-Life Books, *Red Army Resurgent*. Alexandria, VA: Time-Life Books, 1979. The USSR's triumph in clear words and sometimes amazing pictures.

William L. Shirer, *The Rise and Fall of the Third Reich*. New York: Simon & Schuster, 1950. The best-known and arguably the most thorough account of Hitler's Germany from beginning to end by an American newspaper correspondent who witnessed much of it firsthand. Over a thousand pages, but worth the reading.

John J. Vail, *World War II: The War in Europe*. San Diego: Lucent Books, 1991. Clear, accurate, readable, and brief, this book makes an excellent introduction to World War II for young readers.

Gerhard L. Weinberg, *A World at Arms: A Global History of World War II*. Cambridge, England: Cambridge University Press, 1994. This serviceable overview covers most of the bases although the scope will not allow for much detail.

Robert Wernick and the Editors of Time-Life Books, *Blitzkrieg*. New York: Time-Life, 1976. Perhaps the most action-filled book in this series, this book details the how, when, where, and why of Germany's early victories.

Works Consulted

John Erickson, *The Road to Stalingrad: Stalin's War with Germany.* Vol. 1. New York: Harper & Row, 1975. An excellent book, but with its depth and detail it is not a good starting point.

B. H. Liddell Hart, *History of the Second World War.* New York: G. P. Putnam's Sons, 1970. Similar in strengths and weaknesses to Weinberg's *A World at Arms.*

Walther Kirchner, *Russian History.* 7th ed. New York: HarperCollins, 1991. A useful book for background reading because it briefly covers the entire span of Russian history in a straightforward text.

Earl F. Ziemke, *Stalingrad to Berlin: The German Defeat in the East.* Washington, DC: The U.S. Army Center of Military History, 1968. Detailed account of Russia's victory for those who want to know more.

Index

Academy of Fine Arts, 19
appeasement, policy of, 23, 31
Attlee, Clement, 85
Axis
  formed by Berlin and Rome, 33
  joined by Japan, 36
  joined by Bulgaria, Hungary, and Romania, under presure, 36

Balck, Hermann, 72
Barbarossa. *See* Operation Barbarossa
Battle of Britain (the Blitz), 34–36
Battle of Stalingrad
  beginning of end for Hitler, 9–10
  casualties, 77–78
  importance of, 9–10
  Operation Star (mop-up action), 80–81
  see also Operation Blau; Uranus
beer hall putsch, 21
Big Three meetings, 85
Blau. *See* Operation Blau
the Blitz (battle of Britain), 34–36
blitzkrieg, 34, 78
Bolsheviks, 18
  nationalized Russia, 15
  revolution, 12
  sued for peace in World War I, 14
casualties
  American military deaths, 87
  at Stalingrad, 77–78
  German losses, 87
  Russian
    civilians in World War II, 42, 87
    total military deaths, 87
Chamberlain, Neville, 23, 31
Chemist's Shop (Russian stronghold), 65
Chuikov, Vasily Ivanovich, 79
  defense of Stalingrad, 62–65
  personal characteristics, 62–63
Churchill, Winston, 31, 34–35, 76, 85

Commissar Order, 40
communism, brief history, 13
Communist Party, 13

Dragan, Anton Kuzmich, 59
Dunkirk, evacuation of, 32
Dzhugashvili, Iosif Vissarionovich. *See* Stalin, Joseph

Eisenhower, Dwight, 49
Esser (German sergeant), 60–61

Fascists, 13
France, falls to Hitler, 31–34
Franco, Francisco, 18, 23, 33

Germany
  attempted campaign in Kursk salient, 83–84
  blitzkrieg into Poland, 26–28
  captures France with end run, 31–34
  declared war on United States, 45
  invades Scandinavian countries, 28, 31
  mutual nonagression pact with USSR, 18, 25
  pre–World War II expansion, 23
  surrender ends World War II, 87
  see also Battle of Stalingrad; Hitler, Adolf; Operation Blau
Göring, Hermann, 21, 24, 34
  broken promises, 69–71
Greece, invaded by Italy, then Germany, 36
Guderian, Heinz, 44, 84
guerrilla resistance by USSR, 42

Halder, Franz, 43, 61
Heim, Ferdinand, 66
Hindenburg, Paul von, 22
Hitler, Adolf
  assassination attempt on, 78–79
  Battle of Stalingrad
    was a test of wills with Stalin, 10
    was beginning of end, 9–10
  believed to have committed suicide, 87

bloodless occupations before World War II, 23
Commissar Order, 40
comparisons with Napoléon, 70
defied Treaty of Versailles, 23
disastrous decision in Operation Blau, 52
disregarded generals' advice, 69
early life, 19
failed exam for Academy of Fine Arts, 19
joined National Socialist German Workers Party, 20
led attempt to overthrow Bavarian government, 20–21
imprisoned, 20–21
named chancellor, 22
personal characteristics, 11–12
political objectives, 21–22
rise to power, 18–23
signed pact with USSR, invaded Poland, 25–26
symbolic importance of Stalingrad, 55
World War I experiences, 19
see also Germany; *Mein Kampf*
"Hitler weather," 39
Hoth, Hermann, 57–58, 63
Hube, Hans, 56, 57

il Popolo d'Italia (newspaper), 33
Iron Curtain, 85
Italy
  invaded France, 32–33
  invaded Greece, 36
  see also Mussolini, Benito

Japan
  advances in Pacific, 75
  attack on Pearl Harbor, 45
  joined Axis, 36
Ju-87 Stuka dive-bomber, 30
Junker 52s, 70

Katyusha rockets, 73
Kharkov debacle (by Stalin), 48–50
Khrushchev, Nikita, 62, 77
  as political commissar, 49–50
Kursk salient, German campaign, 83–84

lebensraum (living space), 21, 23, 36, 42
Lenin, Vladimir Ilich, 9, 14–16
  established first communist government, 13
Leningrad, 9
  one objective of Operation Barbarossa, 38
  under siege, refused to surrender, 45
List, Wilhelm, 52, 54, 57
Ludendorff, Erich, 21

MacArthur, Douglas, 49
Maginot Line, 28, 31–32
Malenkov, Georgy, 50
Manstein, Erich von
  attempt to save Germans at Stalingrad, 71–73
    final maneuvers during battle, 80–82
maps
  German army trapped at Stalingrad, 72
  Operation Barbarossa, 38
  Operation Blau
    first stage, 53
    Russian counteroffensive, 68
Marx, Karl, 13, 16
Marxism, 14
master race, as espoused by Hitler, 22
Mein Kampf (My Struggle, Hitler), 21, 36
  advocated idea of lebensraum, 21
  a master race, 21
  foretold invasion of USSR, 36
  written in prison, 21
Molotov, Vyacheslav, 53
Molotov Cocktail, 53
Montgomery, Bernard, 49, 75
Moscow Solution. See Uranus
Munich beer hall putsch, 21
Mussolini, Benito, 13, 32, 36
  became dictator in Italy, 20
  brief biography, 33
  death, 33
"mutual assistance" pacts, as means of control, 31
mutual nonagression pact (USSR/Germany, 1939), 18

Napoléon, comparison with Hitler, 70
"The National Question and Social Democracy" (Stalin), 15
National Socialist German Workers Party became known as Nazis, 20
  Hitler joined, 20
Nazism, brief history, 13
Nicholas II (tsar of Russia), 12

Operation Barbarossa (three-pronged attack on USSR), 37–45
  early success, 39–40
  failed to achieve objectives, 45
  guerrilla resistance, 42
  Hitler's Commissar Order, 40
  "Hitler weather" and, 39
  Leningrad under siege, 45
  map, 38
  propaganda for, 37–38
  Russian winter the deciding factor, 46–47
  Soviet resistance develops, 40–44
  Stalin
    scorched-earth policy, 42–43
    unaccountable silence, 42
  USSR superior manpower and supplies, 43–45, 47–48
Operation Blau (Caucasus offensive), 46, 50–61
  beginnings, 50–51
  camels used to haul oil, 54
  the Chemist's Shop and the Red House (Russian strongholds), 65
  Hitler's disastrous decision, 52
  Hoth's brilliant maneuver, 58
  map of first stage, 53
  mice damage German tanks, 66
  snipers, 60
  Soviets' early tactics, 51–52
  street-to-street warfare, 58–59
  surprise resistance, 56–58
  women factory workers manned guns, 56, 57
  see also Uranus
Operation Canned Goods, 27
Operation Star (mop-up action), 80–81

panzers, described, 29
Paulus, Friedrich
  attack/defense of Stalingrad, 50–51, 55–58, 62–66, 70, 77–78
  personal characteristics, 56
  surrenders, 74
Pearl Harbor, Japanese attack on, 45
Petrograd, 9
"Phony War" (France and England declare war on Germany), 28
Poland
  Hitler's plan for lebensraum in, 23, 25
  invaded by Germany, 26–28
Politburo (policy-making body of Bolshevik government), 16
Popov, M. M., 81
Pravda (Truth), 15, 18, 80

RAF (Britain's Royal Air Force), 34–35
Red House (Russian stronghold), 65
Reeder, Red, 11, 13
Reichstag, 23
Reynaud, Paul, 34
Richthofen, Manfred von ("Red Baron"), 24
Richthofen, Wolfram von, 56, 69
Rommel, Erwin, 48, 75–76
  assassination attempt on Hitler, 79
  forced to commit suicide, 79
Roosevelt, Franklin, 32, 76, 85
Royal Air Force (RAF), 34–35
Rundstedt, Gerd von, 39
Russia
  Bolshevik Revolution, 12, 14–15
  World War I and, 12
  see also Stalin, Joseph; Union of Soveit Socialist Republics (USSR)
Russification policy, 17
Russian Revolution (1917), 9

Schulenberg, Friedrich Werner von der, 37
scorched-earth policy by Stalin, 42–43
Seydlitz-Kurzbach, Walter von, 69

"Shrieking Vulture" (the Ju-87 Stuka), 30
Siegfried Line, 28
snipers, 60
Soviet, defined, 15
Soviet-German nonaggression pact, 28
Soviet of the People's Commissars, 15
S.S. (German secret service), 40, 41
Stalin, Joseph, 9, 76, 85
  conferred with Churchill, 77
  converted Russia to full dictatorship, 13
  early life, 15
  early political career, 15
  lobbied for second front, 76
  personal characteristics, 12
  public image after Stalingrad, 79–80
  reign of terror under, 16–18
  rise to limitless power, 15–16
  scorched-earth policy, 42
  Kharkov debacle, 48–50
  unaccountable silence during invasion, 37, 42
Stalingrad
  description and importance, 54–55
  history of name changes, 9
  population before and after battle, 59
  symbolic importance to Hitler, 55
  see also Battle of Stalingrad
Stauffenberg, Klaus von, 79
The Story of the Second World War (Reeder), 11
suicide
  German soldiers, 74
  Hitler, 87
superpowers and cold war are born, 87

T-34 tanks, 47
  at Stalingrad, 63, 66, 71–73, 83
  developed by USSR, 29
Tass, 37
Thorwald, Heinz, 60
Timoshenko, Semyon, 37, 49, 51
Treaty of Versailles, 19

defied by Hitler, 23
Trotsky, Leon, 15–16
Truman, Harry, 85
Tsaritsyn, original name of Stalingrad, 9

Union of Soviet Socialist Republics (USSR), 9
  attacked Finland in Winter War, 31
  casualties
    estimated civilian deaths in World War II, 42
    total military deaths, 87
  invaded Berlin, 87
  invaded Poland, 28
  mutual nonagression pact with Germany, 18, 25
  officially formed, 15
  Russification policy, 17
  slow resistance to invasion, 40–44
  Stalin gains absolute power, 16–18
United Nations, 85
United States
  entered war after Pearl Harbor attack, 45
  massive support for USSR, 47
  Normandy invasion, 86
  offensive after Pearl Harbor, 75
Uranus (Stalingrad counterattack), 64–74
  German army dies, 73–74
  German army trapped at Stalingrad, 69–72
    map, 72
  Hitler disregarded generals' advice, 69
  plans kept secret, 64–65
  relief of Germans attempted, 71–73
  Russian counteroffensive, 68
  shortage of German supplies, 69–71
    first Germans starved to death, 71
  suicide of German soldiers, 74

Vasileysky, Alexander, 64, 67, 79, 84
Vatutin, Nikolai, 66, 67, 68, 81

Volgograd, formerly Stalingrad, 9
von Bock, Fedor, 38, 50, 51, 52, 55
von Leeb, Wilhelm, 38
von Weichs, Maximilian, 52, 55, 56

Winter War (Finland, 1939), 31
women factory workers
  manned guns during battle, 56, 57
World War I, 12
  Bolsheviks sued for peace, 14
  Hitler's experiences, 19
  Treaty of Versailles, 19
World War II
  casualties
    American military deaths, 87
    at Stalingrad, 77–78
    German losses, 87
    Russian civilians, 42, 87
    Russian military deaths, 87
  Pearl Harbor attack forces U.S. entry, 45
World War II, the early war
  Battle of Britain, 34–36
  evacuation of Dunkirk, 32
  events leading to, 23–25
  Germany invades Poland, 26–28
  Germany invades Scandinavian countries, 28, 31
  Germany surrenders, 87
  Greece invaded by Italy, then Germany, 36
  pre-war German expansion, 23
  the "Phony War," 28
  USSR attacks Finland, 31
  USSR invades Poland, 26–28
  see also Battle of Stalingrad

Yelchenko, Fyodor, 74
Yeremenko, A. I., 62, 67, 68, 79

Zaitsev, Vasily, 60
Zhukov, Georgy, 37
  brief biography, 49
  defense of Stalingrad, 62, 64, 67, 78–80, 84
  in Operation Blau, 48, 51

Picture Credits

Cover photo: ITAR-TASS/SOVFOTO

AP/Wide World Photos, 8 (left), 15, 41, 47, 57, 61, 63, 69, 82

Archive Photos, 14, 26, 30, 32, 78

Corbis-Bettmann, 14, 19

Library of Congress, 9, 12, 13, 17, 20, 29, 76

National Archives, 22, 34, 35, 44, 66, 75, 86

Simon Wiesenthal Center, 24

UPI/Corbis-Bettmann, 8 (right), 31, 39, 43, 48, 62, 77

About the Author

Bob Carroll is the author of more than twenty books and over two hundred articles about sports history. His credits include *The Hidden Game of Football* (with John Thorn and Pete Palmer) and *Pro Football: When the Grass Was Real*, the story of the game in the 1960s. He is features editor and writes a regular column for *Oldtyme Baseball News*. He is presently editing the forthcoming *Total Football*, the official National Football League encyclopedia. In the category of historical biography, he has written *The Importance of Napoléon* and *The Importance of Pancho Villa*. In addition to writing, he is a sports artist whose illustrations appear regularly in several national publications. Mr. Carroll lives in North Huntingdon, Pennsylvania.